The Magic of Awareness

The Magic of Awareness

Anam Thubten

Edited by Sharon Roe

Shambhala
Boston & London

Shambhala Publications, Inc.
Horticultural Hall
300 Massachusetts Avenue
Boston, Massachusetts 02115
www.shambhala.com

9 8 7 6 5 4 3

Printed in the United States of America

♾ This edition is printed on acid-free paper that meets the American National Standards Institute Z39.48 Standard.
♲ Shambhala Publications makes every effort to print on recycled paper. For more information please visit www.shambhala.com.

Distributed in the United States by Penguin Random House LLC and in Canada by Random House of Canada Ltd

Library of Congress Cataloging-in-Publication Data
Thubten, Anam.
The magic of awareness / Anam Thubten; edited by Sharon Roe.
p. cm.
ISBN 978-1-55939-392-8 (alk. paper)
1. Religious life—Buddhism.
I. Roe, Sharon (Sharon J.) II. Title.
BQ5410.T575 2012
294.3'444—dc23
2011042227

Wonder,
Who has the magic to make the sun
appear every morning?
Who makes that bird on the elegant tree chirp?

Breath, pulse, music, dew, sunset,
The burning ambers of the fall.
There is unfathomable joy in all that.
Life is a stream.
It flows on its own.

No one knows why we are here.
Stop trying to figure out the great mystery.
The tea in front of you is getting cold.
Drink it.
Enjoy every drop of it.
And dance.
Dance until there is no more dancer,
It is the dance without dancer.
This is how great mystics dance.

Contents

Editor's Preface

THE MAGIC OF AWARENESS is Anam Thubten's second book based on teachings given at Dharmata Foundation, Pt. Richmond, California. A central theme is that enlightenment is always available, even in this very ordinary moment. It is something extraordinary that ordinary people can witness here and now, whenever we are ready. Spiritual awakening can happen to anyone at any time because it is not bound by culture or religion, and its possibility is our birthright.

Rinpoche speaks with startling insight, unflinching honesty, and a great sense of humor. He cuts to the essence, the heart of the matter, drawing from his personal experience of walking the spiritual path, and clarifies subtle, complex points directly, in easily understood language. Rinpoche invites us to fully awaken to the pure, unborn, self-enlightened, unbounded Buddha mind that is already present within us. True spiritual realization, he says, is the experiential understanding of this, and our life's true purpose.

He encourages us to embrace real life rather than the one that exists in our head and is actually nothing more than an accumulation of stories from the past and anticipated, unfulfilled fantasies. Real life, he says, is much more rich and interesting, and it is unfolding right now, here in the present moment. He challenges us to embrace and enjoy it fully.

It is a pleasure and an honor to work with Rinpoche and to present now to a wider audience the profound, illuminating teachings of this devoted man who has dedicated his life to expressing in words and actions messages of authentic love, wisdom, and compassion.

Sharon Roe

CHAPTER ONE

Being Nobody

THERE IS A DIMENSION of reality in which we are nobody and we don't have anything; so there is nothing to lose. It sounds like a total failure since our ego is always trying to be somebody and to have this and that. Yet this turns out to be the highest truth, what is intrinsically so. This benevolent, extraordinary truth, the moment we see it and surrender to it, destroys literally every chain binding us.

There are chains in each of us, a chain of hatred, a chain of fear, a chain of beliefs, a chain of delusion, and so forth. Longchenpa said, "Good concepts are like a golden chain. Bad concepts are like an iron chain. They all equally bind you in the end." So there are a lot of chains in each of us. They constantly torment us and give us unending struggles as well as comfort sometimes too, false comfort. Usually it is the concepts which are like golden chains that give us false comfort. Sometimes, when we become spiritual, we go around collecting belief systems, which simply add more chains in our minds. We collect golden ornaments, forgetting that these spiritual beliefs are just a bunch of golden chains that cannot offer us freedom and unconditional happiness. For this reason Buddha encouraged everybody to enter the enlightened path by taking the most important step which became known as taking refuge. The idea of taking refuge is to completely stop taking refuge in false comfort. False comfort can be ordinary or it can be spiritual, but we completely stop taking refuge in false comfort and turn our attention to an inexhaustible source of freedom. This is the infinite, the oneness, the highest truth, the basic ground of who we are.

A friend who has been meditating for the past two or three years said that she has gone through a very radical transformation. She has changed so much that her friends often don't recognize her. She has been so joyous that she often goes out dancing. She says she has become a dance maniac. She dances so joyously that people sometimes look at her and ask, "Who are you?" Maybe the chains in her consciousness are breaking.

So the highest truth destroys all of the chains. The highest truth where we are nobody and we have nothing is actually a state of our consciousness that is unconditioned. It is our basic ground; it is the primordial mind.  It is the state of reality in which we become nobody and we remain as we are, which is deathless awareness. This is who we are. This is actually our primordial face. The time before we become somebody is called "primordial time" in the Buddhist tantras. Primordial time means the eternal time of primordial purity, which is not actually time in terms of past, present, or future. It is eternal time; it is everlasting time. In that everlasting time we were, as well as we are, and we will be intrinsically luminous awareness. We were, we are, and we will be an inexhaustible treasure of joy and grace, which is who we really are.

There is a funny story told by a very renowned swami from India. One time there was a guru, or master, and his disciple. They both were swamis, renunciants. The master taught the disciple informally. He didn't read texts and he didn't elaborate on commentaries or holy scripture. Instead he taught informally through gestures and examples. The guru always told the disciple, "Don't become somebody. Never become somebody." That was his message. The disciple said that he understood that. One day they set off on a pilgrimage. They traveled together and the guru took him to a royal palace. It was quite a long journey and when they finally arrived they both were exhausted. In the garden of the palace there were cottages. The guru entered one of the cottages and immediately fell asleep. The disciple, imitating his teacher, went to another cottage and fell asleep. They slept peacefully for about a half hour and then the king arrived with his entourage. The king saw these two strange people sleeping in his cottages and he was furious. First he went to the disciple and demanded, "Who are you?" The disciple woke up and saw the wrathful expression on the king's face. He was terrified and he said, "I am a swami." The king said, "You are such a crazy swami!" He grabbed a whip from one of his servants, started beating the disciple, and threw him out of the cottage. Then the king approached the guru. Again he was very furious and demanded, "Who are you?" The guru said, "Hmmmm." He didn't answer. The king shouted loudly, "I asked, who are you?" Again, the guru didn't say anything except "Hmmmm." The king said, "He is a half-wit. He is obviously an idiot. Just take him out of here." Finally, the guru and the disciple met up with each other. The disciple was moaning and groaning. He had pain everywhere because he was injured from the beating. The guru said, "I told you, don't become anybody. You forgot my message and look what has happened to you. I didn't become anybody so I am perfectly fine. You became somebody. You became a swami in that royal cottage and you were punished for that."

This is the problem. We all become somebody from that time of original purity. We become somebody. We become this limited entity, and we pretend to be separate from the oneness, from the source. We pretend that we have fallen from the grace of our original face. We pretend to be a man, a woman, a teacher, a student, a politician, a taxi driver, a good person, a bad person, educated, wealthy, or poor. When we take these masks as our true identity, then an unending struggle takes place. It is like

the ocean forgot that she is this unfathomable, vast sea and ended up believing that she is merely this tiny drop of water. This is what happens in our consciousness and this is what is the prime mover of all of our struggles.

So there is a state of reality as well as consciousness, even in this very moment, in the nowness, in which we actually are nobody and we don't have anything. This sounds very bad. It sounds like total failure, but it is the most beautiful truth that we can ever witness. It is, once again, eternal time or primordial purity. The goal, as well as the purpose of all spiritual practices and endeavors, is not to go somewhere. The goal is not even to go back to some notion of a divine source. The goal is to come here. To come to the very core essence of our being, and to recognize this amazing reality, this supreme truth in which we are nobody and we have nothing.

Everything we think that we possess is merely an illusion. We have a lot of things, material as well as nonmaterial things. We possess a lot in the world of the material. We have countless gadgets and toys. When we look into our consciousness we also have a lot of stuff. We have belief systems and concepts, ideas, guilt, shame, pride, and also conceit. But none of these possessions actually exist in the realm of primordial purity. They only exist in the realm of delusion, in the realm of egoic mind and samsaric consciousness. But this does not mean that we should throw everything out of the window. This is not

saying that we shouldn't play any roles. Of course, we play many roles. We play the role of female and male, the role of teacher and student. These roles are necessary for consciousness to maintain this amazing form called life, called an incarnation, not necessarily reincarnation but incarnation.

So there is a consciousness in each of us that is nobody. It is not American, European, Tibetan, or Chinese. We can discover that consciousness inside that is literally nobody. It goes beyond all the roles and personas we take on in this lifetime. These are what the ego consists of, its life and energy. Our body can be male or female but our consciousness is neither male nor female. This is not proposing a duality between body and mind. This is saying that there is a difference between who we are as an essence and the role we play in this world. Sometimes we play the role of a man, sometimes the role of a woman. Sometimes we are the teacher, sometimes the student, every day we play different roles.

When we play these roles, we are, to a large degree, completely immersed in the very form that we are taking in this transient, fleeting, amazing, beautiful, exquisite incarnation. But when we meditate we open our hearts. We put aside all of our beliefs, our assumptions, our prejudices, and our notions of reality as well. We put aside all of our mental fabrication and without going anywhere, without doing anything, a miracle happens. The miracle is that we have direct contact with that dimension of who we are, the consciousness that Buddha was talking about, the boundless, formless consciousness that is nobody. And yet it is everything. It is Buddha, it is the awareness, the consciousness, the experience that we are, actually, one with everybody. We are one with nirvana and samsara. We are one with the sky as well as the earth.

This consciousness, the consciousness prior to becoming somebody, prior to becoming finite is difficult to describe. It is not a thing and it can be a difficult truth to believe in and to trust in. The most available, closest analogy, as well as what we might call scientific evidence for this consciousness, is actually the presence of a newborn child. When we look into the face of a newborn child what do we see? There is pure innocence. Hospitals have a place with a window where the newborn babies sleep. When we go there, we see a group of people, old and young, staring at the babies. These people are experiencing satori, sudden enlightenment, just looking at the perfection of the newborn children. They forget who they are. Nobody has any problems, nobody hates anybody, and nobody knows who they are anymore. Nobody remembers how much money they have in their bank account and nobody remembers who is their enemy and who is their friend. Everyone is experiencing satori and they will stay there just watching the babies until somebody asks them to leave.

There are many ways of having satori, a sudden awakening to this extraordinary, eternal dimension inside of us. Sometimes simple things work. But the reason people are sometimes drawn to this inexpressible calmness, the wonder of the presence of the newborn child, is because of the innocence in the child. We are all drawn and truly inspired by that innocence. Do we find judgment in that innocence? Is that innocence judging us? Do we judge that innocence? No, there is no judgment in that innocence. We have no concept of the child as European or Tibetan, as black or white. There are no concepts, there is only pure awareness, pure innocence.

So there is this pure, true nature in each of us. In the presence of that we are nobody. We are not finite. We are no longer bound by all of these chains, chains of hope and fear. We are totally fearless as well as loving and compassionate without any causes and conditions. This is the truth that Buddha and wise masters from many traditions have been pointing out. This is actually the goal. This is the goal of the journey and this goal can be actualized even in this very moment, even in this very ordinary moment, in this nowness.

Spiritual masters always encourage us to open our heart, to pray and sit and listen to teachings that are the pure expression of truth, not the expression of ideas and concepts, but the pure expression of the truth. We can listen to those teachings by heart as well as by ear and then soon we will witness this miracle. Then there is a path that we walk and the path is actually fun. That path is to keep remembering that we are this pure consciousness while we are playing a role. And we play our role with such sweetness, kindness, and joy that wherever we go we actually radiate peace and loving-kindness.

CHAPTER TWO

Flipping Our Consciousness

WHEN WE READ some of the ancient Buddhist scriptures, we come across this extraordinary event that describes the Buddha's enlightenment. It is said that the moment Buddha awoke, the earth trembled, and the gods in the heavens celebrated. This is a metaphor, but what it is trying to express is that enlightenment is a miracle. It is the greatest miracle that there is. Life is filled with miracles. When we see the northern lights or a flower blossom right in front of us, these are miracles too, but the greatest miracle is enlightenment. It's a miracle because it allows us to witness a new reality; one that our conditioned mind is not too familiar with. Whereas our conditioned mind is usually familiar with the world of sorrow, the world of concepts and ideas, enlightenment is a world that is free from all limitations, a world that is filled with love, joy, and wisdom.

Enlightenment is a spiritual epiphany that we can all witness. It is an epiphany when conditioned mind dissolves and suddenly we enter into a whole new reality.

Yet it takes just a millisecond to shift from our old frame of mind into this totally new frame of mind. We can use the expression "flipping our consciousness" to describe it. Flipping our consciousness is like flipping a coin. When we flip a coin we simply turn it from one side to the other side. It doesn't take any mental process or any effort to see the other side of the coin. It doesn't take a long time. We can flip our consciousness the same way that we flip a coin and when we do, the other side of our conditioned mind is enlightenment. There are only two states of consciousness, there's no third state. One state of consciousness is enlightened and the other state is not enlightened. That means that either we are deluded or we are completely enlightened. There is no in-between state.

Unenlightened consciousness is not always dreadful and filled with bitterness and misery. Actually, sometimes unenlightened consciousness can be quite wholesome and it can be very juicy too. Falling in love with someone can be quite ecstatic when the other person responds. That's why we long for romance. Imagine that a great romance is happening in our life right now. Perhaps we feel that our lover is the epitome of all perfections. It may not be true at all, but for us everything becomes magic. The truth is that this whole experience takes place in our deluded consciousness and perhaps we never suspect that there is anything wrong. Then, after everything falls apart, we wonder how that could happen. So we can see that it's possible to entertain ourselves endlessly. The problem is that it ends in disappointment.

True happiness comes into being only when we are awakened from that unenlightened consciousness. Such spiritual awakening can happen right where we are. As a matter of fact, it never happens anywhere else. There are two approaches that can initiate that sudden awakening. Both of these approaches are immediate ways to flip our consciousness. The first approach is to let go of all of our mind's creation. We can let all of our mind's fictitious stories die and exit from the world of suffering, misery, attachment, fantasy, and obsession. We can just drop it all, let it all go, and that works. But there is another approach and that is to remember that we are all born newly in each and every moment. We can let ourselves be born for the first time in this moment and begin a new human life with so much wonder and marvel. We can make a clean break with our old identity, as if that was never us in the first place. When we talk about our past, we can imagine that we are talking about someone that we knew a long time ago, but have not kept in touch with lately. We know that when we are born, we are perfectly innocent and free from all flaws. This spiritual birth can only occur through the death of the old self. That's why there is a saying in the Zen tradition: "One must die some day on the meditation cushion."

It is beautiful when we truly realize that we are born

in this very moment for the first time in human history. When we look at the face of a young child, we often feel a sense of inspiration and hope because the child doesn't have a lot of history. We are inspired because the child's life is totally full of possibility and potential. However, when we reach a certain age, we sometimes feel that there are no more possibilities in our life. We feel that life is already over, even though it is not. We feel that we are already reaching the end or at least the middle of our life. We may be having a midlife crisis because there are not many possibilities. We feel that we have made mistakes and that we are not perfect. But this is simply a defense launched by the ego to ward off that great miracle that is ready to happen at any given moment. We use the expression "It's too late for me." But enlightenment, this great miracle, is not too late for any of us. It is not too late because enlightenment is not an achievement that requires a lot of effort or preparation. It does not require special skills. In the end it doesn't require anything.

When our heart is completely open, then that spiritual epiphany, that great miracle, can actually happen. Opening the heart is a beautiful expression. It is not conceptual. It is so nonconceptual that the intellect cannot understand what it means. We have an intellectual, rational intelligence, which we use to figure things out in our everyday life. But sometimes we use this conceptual intelligence in relationship to spiritual truths. We try to figure out transient things like supreme emptiness, oneness, and so forth. Opening the heart is not an intellectual process and that's why the rational, intellectual mind can't understand how to experience it. We have to go beyond our intellectual mind to open our heart.

An open heart can only be experienced when we go beyond the realm of the intellectual mind. Our thinking mind is beautiful; it is a gift. So, thanks to the thinking mind, but there is a whole other level of reality that the thinking mind cannot figure out, no matter how hard it tries. Lama Mipham, one of the most enlightened Tibetan masters, said, "I am so exhausted with the fact that this thinking mind is always searching for the truth." That's a beautiful phrase, which eloquently expresses the fact that the thinking mind cannot realize the ultimate truth. There is an old metaphor which says, "You cannot get butter by squeezing sand." Somebody can spend years and years on the beach squeezing sand. When you ask them what they are doing, they say they are looking for butter and trying to squeeze it out of the sand. We all know that we could keep squeezing the dry sand for a thousand eons and never get even one drop of butter, because sand is obviously void of butter. But just like that, the thinking mind tries to figure out the ultimate truth, and it never can because it is the wrong tool.

Our thinking mind is always trying to figure out things that are beyond it. Boundless love, Buddha mind, ultimate surrender, the death of ego, these all go beyond the thinking mind. When we seek the highest truth by learning theories this is a clear sign that the thinking mind is engaged in things that are beyond it. At that moment we should feel totally exhausted because we are once again trying to get butter by squeezing dry sand.

Opening the heart is a different matter. It doesn't think or strategize. Instead it just goes about melting this mountain of ice within. Opening the heart in the ultimate sense wants nothing. It has no ambitions. It is the most courageous expression of the human heart. It is simply about losing all of our ego's defensiveness. Sometimes we don't know how to open our heart. Then we can go inside and look for what is preventing us from opening our heart. It might be doubt, fear, resistance, or anything else for that matter. Usually those things dissolve when we acknowledge them. Most thieves run away when we shine light on their faces and, in the same way, those obstructions can only function in the darkness of unawareness. Machik Labdron, the most revered Tibetan saint, taught that the most powerful way to overcome inner obstructions is to relate to them as honored guests. We invite them into our home and feed them. Soon they all leave. This all has to do with acknowledging them in the light of awareness.

The best word I can use to describe the experience of a totally open heart is "devotion." The Buddhist master

Asanga said that the truth can only be realized through devotion. The devotion that he was speaking about was not some kind of conceptual devotion based on projections and illusions, but enlightened devotion. Enlightened devotion is actually love, a form of trust. But it is love that has no object; trust that has no object. Love, courage, trust, and bliss are available to the extent that we lose all of our defensiveness. Lose even the last defensiveness, which is the conceptual mind's desire to figure out enlightenment. It is the thought that we want to get, or acquire, enlightenment in the same way that we want to get or acquire a car. We want to get a lot of things in life, and now we want to get enlightenment.

The conceptual mind's desire to get enlightenment is a defensiveness which wards off enlightenment itself. When we open our heart, we lose all defensiveness, all fear, all insecurity, all desire, all wanting, and all conceptualizing. We lose it all and we are as innocent and pure as if we were born in this very moment without any history, without any attachment to anything. We are free from everything and we are like an innocent child once again. The mind of a child is free from all concepts, all ideas, and all fears, free from all strategies. It is just pure trust, pure love. It is so nonconceptual that in the end there are no perfect words to describe it.

The true meaning of opening our heart is that we no longer have fear of losing anything. It is a form of surrender, yet such surrender has no object. It is not like we are surrendering to something. What we surrender are our hopes and fears, and an investment in our misery. When we have reached the final point of that surrender there is nothing that we want to hold on to. The only thing that happens is this effortless and sudden opening of a dimension of our consciousness that is vast and joyous. This surrender can happen in an instant, like the blink of an eye. It is literally like flipping the consciousness to its other side right there. It is a miraculous transformation from a contracted state to an expansive state of consciousness. Usually surrender has a meaning which connotes weakness and defeat. On the battlefield, raising the white flag is a sign of surrender which means that we have lost.

The surrender that I am talking about here is a demonstration of wisdom and triumph. We just stop building the wall of inner conflict and relax into what is. Everything turns out to be perfect in its imperfection when we allow things to be as they are. There are two states of consciousness, one enlightened and one deluded. They are like two sides of a coin. We can flip our consciousness in the same way we flip a coin. It's just like flipping the channel on our TV. It takes only a moment and there is no special skill required. We don't need a long time to prepare for the task either. We can simply exhale and just let go of our entire story line, the one we are taking so seriously.

One of my dear friends, a great spiritual teacher,

uses the expression "chill out." It sounds very simple but that's all we need to do. We don't really have to be particularly spiritual or serious to enter the world of enlightenment. We don't even have to be prepared. We just relax our shoulders and let go. With divine ease we lose all of our defensiveness, and all of our strategies which are never going to work out anyway. We just let it all go and before we know it we feel new in that moment. The person who was complaining about life and trying to figure out enlightenment no longer exists.

If we hold a strong intention to let go of all of our thoughts, we can witness our consciousness changing, just like flipping a coin. This also happens whenever we focus our attention toward simple things or events in our immediate surrounding, like the flow of breath, the sound of a dog barking, or even the stillness of the chair. Remember, the universe is opening countless doors for us. We just lose everything, and when we do we suddenly discover that we are residing in this new dimension of mind and we can dance in the ground of joy, love, bliss, and trust.

This experience of flipping our consciousness can happen with the simplest method. The method must be immediate. If it is complicated, we may be carried away by what we are trying to resolve before we free ourselves from the entanglement. The radical master Tilopa said, "Inquire into the mind using the mind itself. All concepts will cease and you will see what the nature of mind is."

Just like that, the method that Tilopa taught is also central to many of the nondogmatic teachings of the Buddhist masters. What he is saying is that if you just take a moment to stop the mind from constantly perpetuating habitual patterns, you will enjoy witnessing the highest form of freedom in that moment. Mind's habit stops in that inquiry without anything further to be done. This inquiry has no esoteric meaning. It is a sudden entering into your own nonconceptual awareness. This is a method of flipping the consciousness from the side of confusion to the side of clarity.

The other side of consciousness is already enlightened. In Buddhist language, reaching enlightenment is called "arriving at the other shore." That other shore is not so far from here. You will be able to cross the ocean of suffering and reach the other shore, the shore of freedom, with miraculous speed.

CHAPTER THREE

Awakening to Our True Nature

ONE OF THE CENTRAL messages in the Buddhist tradition is that the quintessential nature of mind is already pure and immaculate. It is already enlightened. That is what is known in Buddhism as luminous mind. It is always residing in each of us as the indestructible dimension of who we are. Yet it is not to be mistaken as a sacred object or some kind of grandiose, mystical entity. It can be immediately discovered when we stop entertaining concepts about it. Maybe that is why Buddha explained the truth with language of negation. That is also why he said the truth is too subtle to teach. Up to now the human mind has the propensity to often miss what is subtle and profound. It tends to be attracted to what is coarse. When it contemplates higher realities, it tries to figure them out through beliefs and images. So this notion of luminous mind is very subtle. It can never be realized by theorizing about it or believing in it. On the other hand, we can be awakened to it in every instant if we allow for it.

Most spiritual people are looking for something, and most of the time we believe that what we are looking for is outside of ourselves. But ultimately what we are seeking is this unborn, already self-enlightened, unbounded Buddha mind, and it is already present within each of us. This pure, immaculate dimension of our mind is dwelling in the mind-stream of all of us and true spiritual realization is the experiential understanding of this. There is only one mind, but there are two states of mind, the conditioned mind and the unconditioned mind. We live in our conditioned mind most of the time. Meditation practice is a tool for becoming aware of the luminous mind, which is the unconditioned mind. One of the purposes of meditation is to become aware of the fact that we are living in our conditioned mind most of the time. Then we need to know how to get from there to the realm of our unconditioned mind. That's what meditation practice is all about.

Our mind is consciousness, our sense of being, our sense of life. Mind has this extraordinary ability to think, analyze, label, judge, and experience. When we look into our mind, we see that most of the time we are living in the realm of the conditioned mind. The word for "conditioned mind" in the Tibetan language has the connotation that the conditioned mind is something temporary, something that doesn't belong to the primordial ground of being. It is something that is ready to be dissolved or wiped away, just like the dust on the mirror or a cloud in the sky. The condition is merely an inner obscuration, something that obscures our true nature. The conditions obscuring our mind are not permanent.

If we honestly look inside, we may see right away both conditioned and unconditioned mind. We will also see how much we live in conditioned mind, which is run by thoughts, ideas, and perceptions. Isn't it true that we are constantly experiencing a sense of basic dissatisfaction? It is the very basis of human suffering, which is grounded in ignorance, yet it is almost the normal state of our consciousness. There are many forms of dissatisfaction. Some of them are obvious and some of them are very hidden. Most of the time whatever we are experiencing is merely a mental habit. Fear is a mental habit, so is hatred, and so is this ongoing sense of dissatisfaction. We are dissatisfied with the way we look, with what we have, dissatisfied with others, and so forth. We can be quite dissatisfied spiritually too. Dissatisfaction can pretty much dominate every level of our consciousness. Sometimes wanting to be enlightened, wanting to become holier can be a form of dissatisfaction. It is a spiritual dissatisfaction. This kind of wanting is very different from the spiritual aspiration that is taught as a doorway to enlightenment in many spiritual traditions, because the latter doesn't want anything. It's the total willingness to let go of everything.

Sometimes we have this sudden experience of being very free. It's like we have somehow stumbled into the garden of paradise where suddenly everything becomes clear. We no longer have any doubt about what the truth is, about what our true nature is. There is no longer any confusion, no longer any delusion. There is no longer any exertion in relation to anything. Everything becomes radically clear. This kind of epiphany happens when we allow ourselves to fall from the thinking mind into the heart. The process has the quality of letting go of all of the mental contractions without any more struggling. Usually letting go is a very hard thing for human beings to do. This may have to do with our deep fear that if we just let go of everything, we will lose control over our life. To the ego, it looks like taking our hands off of the steering wheel while the car is moving. It can be more chilling than exciting.

When we allow ourselves to fall into the heart, letting go happens on its own. So there is no longer "I" who is trying hard to either hold on or let go. Such luminous experience can unfold in this very ordinary moment because it is the natural state of our mind. Enlightenment is possible because it is already in each of us; it is the natural state of our mind. If enlightenment were not the natural state of our mind, then enlightenment would be a result, the fruition of a long and arduous process. But it is not a spiritual trophy that we can attain by being smart or by working hard. It is not an award or a reward. It is already the intrinsic state of our mind right now, as it is.

What are we waiting for to be awakened to this

luminous mind that is already our true nature? We know that there is this divine river flowing next to us. We can walk in and drink the water instead of being tormented by thirst. To be awakened to this state of who we are is the only goal of all spiritual practices. This means that the goal of all spiritual practices is not plural, they have the same goal, which is to be awakened to our true nature. It doesn't really matter whether we take another eon or another ten years or another moment. All that matters is that in the end we arrive at this very last point, which is to fully and completely see our true nature. The point is not to conceptualize or intellectualize this, but to experience this beautiful reality.

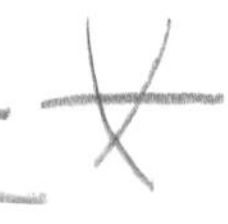

True realization in Buddhism is called "the great seeing." It is where we can see our true nature in the same way we see the faces of our friends, or the people sitting around us, or our own hand in front of our eyes. Such realization is something we can invite in, not something that we can manufacture. We can manufacture many things, including beautiful, ecstatic spiritual experiences. In Tibetan the word *nyam* is used to describe these beautiful experiences that are transient, ephemeral, and lacking in love and true wisdom. It can sometimes be a little bit blissful, but deceptive. However, one thing we cannot manufacture is enlightenment. That is something we cannot manufacture. It actually happens in that realm of seeing our true nature. Then liberation happens. One of the keys, the secret to realizing liberation, is to stop searching and rest in the natural state of mind.

This, of course, can sometimes be quite a confusing message because we cannot really find anything unless we look for it. We can't even find a cup of coffee if we don't look for it. It is not likely that someone will just come to us and hand us a cup of coffee. Even to have just a cup of coffee we have to go out, find a place to park the car, walk to the coffeehouse, and so forth. In this lifetime, as far as this rational mind remembers, everything is achieved and actualized by exerting a tremendous sense of effort, looking, seeking. So the rational mind can be quite confused and perplexed when we are told that the secret key to the discovery of liberation is actually not looking for it anymore. But we cannot look for it because this is not something that we can manufacture. It has to happen on its own when there is an auspicious synchronicity, when there is the right receptivity, when there is the right vantage point in our consciousness, then it happens. So liberation happens naturally in the realm of direct seeing. When our true nature, that primordially self-enlightened state of who we are, is seen, completely seen, not conceptualized but seen, tasted, then liberation is already there.

Liberation is already dancing on the stage, or the platform, of our consciousness. How can we experience that right now? Is there a method? Actually there are many methods. One method is expressed in this very old saying: "Rest in the natural state of mind." This method is powerful, dynamic, and transformative. "Rest," of course, has many meanings, but here "rest" does not mean simply ordinary rest. It does not mean just sitting on the sofa with our feet on the coffee table. Not that kind of resting, but a deep resting. Here resting means stopping all of mind's effort, including the effort of seeking, meditating, analyzing, and trying to hold on to something. It isn't trying to get rid of or achieve something. We just let go of all of mind's effort and be in the natural state of mind and we don't have to figure out what that is. That's the good news. We are no longer the responsible agent who is going to make sure that enlightenment is going to arise on time. That's a big relief, isn't it?

In the morning we see that the sun is shining. When we see the light coming from the shoulder of the eastern mountain, are we the agent responsible for making sure that the sun rises on time? No. In the same way, we don't have to take care of this enlightenment business anymore. In that place of no more searching, we are totally resting without even the slightest sense of exertion. Then, believe it or not, enlightenment shines. Conditioned mind drops away without really making a big fuss once we know how to let liberation come to us by simply resting, deeply resting.

Deeply resting is the point where we are no longer looking for anything else. As long as there is an act of searching for God or truth or eternal self, it is not only that we haven't found it; we are actually moving away from it with great speed. In that deep resting a beautiful stillness arises, which is the vantage point from which we can have a glimpse of the luminous mind and finally merge with it. Many people in the East became renunciants and lived far from worldly distractions to be in that stillness. We don't have to become renunciants to deepen our relationship with that stillness. As our love for this stillness keeps growing, we find many moments every day to dive into it. Soon nothing from the outside has the power to distract us from it. As a matter of fact, everything serves as a gate to enter into it.

Let's wake up to the fragility of human existence. There is no certainty that we will be here tomorrow. What is the point of prolonging our suffering? Can we live with more love and joy? The answer does not lie in having the best technique or the most knowledge, but in our inborn ability to awaken to our true nature, the luminous mind within.

CHAPTER FOUR

Enlightenment as an Ordinary Human Experience

SOMETIMES WE WONDER what the purpose of life is. Usually when we ask this question we are disillusioned. Life seems tiresome, and we are not looking into various ideas about that because we have this deep sense of not succeeding at it. There are some who find deep solace in lofty religious ideas about life. Such psychological comfort will last until its foundation begins to shake. When we come to that point, the same discomforting question about the purpose of life arises again. Whenever that happens, what at first seems to be an insurmountable crisis can turn into a door to freedom, if we take the opportunity.

In the end, there is no perfect answer to this dilemma except the transcendence of the whole thing. This is like leaving a house that is on fire instead of trying to remodel it. This whole business of seeking and holding on to any notions of life's purpose is the work of a mind that is not awakened to the truth. In the absence of both the confusion of not knowing life's purpose and attachment to thinking that one knows the meaning of life's purpose lies the realization which is called enlightenment.

There are countless descriptions of what enlightenment is. Some of them can be hilarious if taken literally. They can make us feel that we will never get it. On top of that, many religious traditions claim that they alone have the key to it. Many people have resigned themselves to the fact that they will not get enlightenment in this lifetime, but sometime in a very vague, distant future, sometime in the hereafter. As long as it is postponed into some future it cannot help anybody get out of misery. It is like a starving person sitting in front of very delicious food and looking around for something to eat.

First let's come to the conclusion that enlightenment is actually possible, here and now. It's something extraordinary and ordinary people can witness it. Everyone, men, women, children, educated people, uneducated people, everyone can witness it because it is nothing more than waking up from a dreamlike reality to what is true. In that moment of waking, love and joy blossom because the foundation of fear and contraction dissolves. It gives us the ultimate confidence that overrides all forms of insecurity. But this confidence is a strange one, because it can only be found in letting go of all forms of security. This truth is both beautiful and unsettling.

A good description of enlightenment would be the state of not having anything to lose or to gain in this or any other world. It is the groundless ground, the place where there is no longer any refuge. It is the refugeless refuge, the point of peace that is devoid of all duality. This might not sound very enticing, yet it would be the most amazing miracle a human being can witness. For the egoic mind, enlightenment is simply seeing the unknown. One of ego's main occupations is to turn the unknown into the known. There is no longer the duality between known and unknown in the highest spiritual awakening; they are both domains of the mind. Enlightenment is simply directly seeing the truth without mind's distortion, clear like the palm of your hand. The truth that we are talking about here is not truth in the conventional sense, rather it is the changeless truth, which is already there prior to the mind. It is *paramartha satya*, the ultimate truth.

There are lots of definitions of what enlightenment is. Sometimes it is described as eternal liberation, the divine nature of everything. It also means the direct seeing of the truth. It seems that the most simple and clear way to define it is to call it spiritual awakening. This is how Buddha defines what enlightenment is. Having said that, spiritual awakening doesn't happen because we are spiritual or because we have been engaged in various spiritual disciplines. When done with the right intention, spiritual disciplines offered by religious traditions have tremendous benefit. This is why Buddha said, "Mind is the forerunner of all things." Done with the wrong intention, even those beautiful spiritual practices become only a driving force for further entanglement in the world of concepts and rigid belief systems. Wanting any form of divine security and solace can be a wrong intention because we are still seeking to preserve our illusions.

Imagine we believe that there is a personal savior out there. It will put our fears to sleep and calm our insecurities. Our mind would have a hard time questioning it. In general, it can be very frightening to see things we used to believe in crumble and fall apart, especially when there is nothing to replace them.

One time a couple that I had never met before attended a retreat. As far as I was able to tell, they were extremely openhearted and committed to waking up. They were the kind of people I like to call natural-born bodhisattvas. After the retreat I received letters from them. The woman said that she was happier than ever. Her husband, on the other hand, had a different reaction. His formal notions of reality began to dissolve one after the other, so he got a little bit scared. The more we resist our personal illusions, the more painful the process of inner awakening is. The moment resistance is given up, the process of inner awakening can be fun and effortless. The root of resistance is fear of death, not physical death, but death of the illusion of a separate self.

True spiritual awakening can happen to anyone, at any time, because it is not bound to culture or religion. It is potentially available as our universal birthright. Buddha saw this potential in everyone. He broke through the rigid Hindu caste system to demonstrate that truth. He invited men and women from every caste into his sangha, or community, and many people woke up to the truth during his lifetime. Some Buddhist teachers predicted that more people will wake up now than ever before in human history. This means that enlightenment can be like the wildflowers that blossom everywhere in spring. Sometimes when we are in the country we notice a field completely covered with wildflowers. It seems like the whole earth has been invaded by wildflowers and they are popping up everywhere, beyond control. Enlightenment is like that sometimes. It pops up in the consciousness of hundreds and thousands of people when there is a collective readiness and pure surrender.

So enlightenment is everything our heart longs for—love, freedom, joy, peace, and meeting our true nature. Enlightenment satisfies whatever we are searching for. Nothing is missing. But remember, it is not a religious phenomenon. It is simply reclaiming our basic sanity by not continuing the big dream of duality. When we lose the big dream, we lose the whole abundance of suffering. That is all we lose. It is not like we stopped suffering temporarily; rather, we began cutting the root of all suffering.

Buddhism sometimes uses a metaphor which says that enlightenment is like walking into a paradise, even though Buddhism does not assert an external paradise. Every culture has a notion of paradise. Paradise is a realm of utter goodness, beauty, joy, and bliss. Buddhism teaches that there is paradise but it does not exist anywhere outside of ourself. Paradise is the awakened mind. Many masters have said that paradise is actually pure perception. Pure perception is this enlightened mind, which is free from all forms of delusion. Here "pure" means free from all delusion because delusion is the root of this very world we are trying to transcend on the spiritual path. The world we are trying to transcend is not the physical world of air, sunlight, and ocean. After all, that world, even with all of its problems, is an amazingly beautiful world. Our problem is with the world that mind has constructed. Can we see that there is a mental world that we have created somewhere in our consciousness? It is a mind-created world that we have been living in forever. When we open our eyes, we see the outer world. We can walk outside near the ocean for just ten or twenty minutes and we see a beautiful world with sand, rocks, and waves; the ocean is singing a song. It is a beautiful world. There is nothing wrong with that world. It is perfect, sacred in itself.

The world that we must transcend is the world that mind has constructed. That world has lots of problems, lots of drama, lots of stories, and lots of suffering. It's a forever spinning wheel of painfulness, agony, and so forth. We all have a desire to transcend this world. Many people get into spiritual practices in order to transcend that world, because ultimately it is just a world of sorrow, confusion, and limitation even though now and then there are some fun moments. There are very poor ways of transcending this mind's world. Sometimes we hibernate in exalted states of spiritual consciousness. Sometimes we go to a theater and watch a movie, which helps us transcend mind's world too. Going to see a movie can be a form of religious observance because we forget ourselves. For a moment we forget all of our problems and have a sense of transcendence. We see people at movie theaters with golden-colored popcorn. They have big smiles on their faces. They seem to have access to some kind of religious experience, some kind of transcendence, but it is a temporary, false transcendence. Believe it or not, much of the time when people come to temples, ashrams, and churches, it's not that different from going to a big movie theater. This is quite sad but it is also the truth.

Many of us have the desire to transcend the world that we have constructed out of delusion, the world we are stuck with, the world of pain and sorrow. This is a divine desire that lies at the core of our spiritual as well as our worldly endeavors. We all want to be free. We all want to alleviate this ongoing sense of being confused, lost, and engaged in this endless struggle. If we have a desire to go beyond this world of limitations, we must remember that such a world is not out there, it is merely the state of our consciousness. The world that many spiritual people are trying to transcend is actually inside. It is not a true reality. It is a provisional reality, a reality that ego has constructed, a dreamlike reality. It is a reality that we are always trying desperately to transcend or hold on to. Sometimes we are so fed up with this world that we want to take a fantastic ride into the galaxy of altered states of consciousness. We want to forget all of our problems and drink the pure nectar of eternal bliss.

The heart of the matter is this. We have to keep going back inside, realizing that what we want to transcend is not outside, it is in each of us. It is simply a mental world, even though it has been serving as the ground of our reality, the notion of life we are embracing. In deep meditation we can reach a point where we can clearly recognize that our previous notions of reality are nothing more than a conglomeration of concepts, beliefs, thoughts, and memories. In that extraordinary realization, everything we believe to be true vanishes. We suddenly realize that we have been watching a movie, a movie of life, a movie of dreamlike reality. If we want to realize what true reality is, all we have to do is simply let go of our current reality. Then reality is already realized. This sounds like one of those mind-torturing paradoxes, doesn't it?

The real question is this: Are we enjoying our current reality right now or not? If we are enjoying reality, then remember that it will not last a long time. It's like an ice cream cone. It won't last forever. Enjoying reality is like enjoying ice cream. It's delicious but sooner or later it will be gone. When we look closely, we know this. But sometimes we are enjoying our current reality so much that our mind convinces us that it will last. Our consciousness is deceived by beautiful illusions. It says, "I'm getting this. I'm getting that. I'm successful. I'm feeling great. I have realized the self. I must be enlightened." These are beautiful realities, but remember there is no true reality. It is better to drop all notions of reality instead of going through the painstaking analysis of trying to figure out the difference between reality and nonreality.

Of course the mind loves analysis. It can spend ten years or more just trying to figure out the distinction between reality and nonreality. The mind can say, "I'm on a spiritual path, trying to solve the greatest mystery, the distinction between reality and nonreality. And the day I realize this, I'm going to achieve that grand, heavenly reward, enlightenment." The mind can be very tricky. But the truth is that mind can get lost in an unending analysis. Many spiritual masters say that a better way is to just drop every notion of reality that we are holding on to: life-death, suffering-happiness, attainment-nonattainment, purity-nonpurity, past-future, success-failure.

The highest level of meditation is transcendent wisdom, or *prajnaparamita*. It is a state of pure awareness, a state of luminous consciousness, a state of wisdom in which all notions of reality have been dissolved—birth, death, everything has been transcended. That is the highest level of meditation; that is pure awareness.

There's not much we can do when we don't know how to just drop this illusion of duality. Sometimes we just sit. Meditation is the art of simply sitting in silence. Sitting means just sit, just rest, just be. Let everything be as it is. When we know how to let everything be as it is, then we don't have to try and be some kind of divine terminator attempting to destroy the world of delusion and sorrow. The world of delusion and sorrow is already falling apart and disappearing on its own. It sounds simple but it is also subtle. We just let everything be just as it is. Once we know that, we know everything. We have unlocked the secret to enlightenment. To sit actually means to just let everything be as it is, and let the world of ideas, concepts, and sorrow dissolve on its own, which always happens. That is the highest technique.

This technique is very subtle. It doesn't work unless there is a burning desire to wake up to the truth, right here and right now. Whenever we see the truth, we will be shocked to see that it has been here all the time. There is an art of inquiry that has been taught in many traditions in various styles, methodologies, formulas, and formats that have been developed over time. Masters have suggested, "Look to see where the mind is. Inquire into whether the mind has an origin or not, whether the mind has a location or not, whether the mind has a source into which it dissolves or not." The format is not so important. When we don't know how to go beyond our notions of reality, when we don't know how to jump into the ocean of love and joy, then sometimes the only thing we can do is to invite this supreme inquiry. Quite simple, isn't it?

In that spirit of inquiry sometimes big openings happen. Sometimes all resistance just falls apart, and we suddenly feel that nothing is blocking our consciousness. Suddenly mind stops fabricating false stories about what reality is. In that undeluded ground of consciousness we will find a true wisdom eye, awakened mind that sees timeless truth.

CHAPTER FIVE

The Art of Enjoying Life

ONE OF THE timeless messages of the Buddha is that human life is extremely short and precious. That is true for all of us regardless of our age. Time is always running out. Life is like the dew on the grass in the morning, it is extremely short. This metaphor tells us that human life is fragile and at the same time exquisitely beautiful in its impermanent nature. Like a sunset or a rainbow, it escapes any attempt to hold on to it, and therefore life should be held as sacred and precious. Sometimes we contemplate its mystery and consider if there is a purpose behind it.

Knowing that life is extremely short and precious, we sometimes get carried away by our desire to do something meaningful with our life. To worry about life being meaningful is a little bit like worrying about insomnia. The more we worry, the more sleep escapes us. In the end, it's often best to forget our grandiose ideas. It has been said that to practice true spirituality is to forget oneself. Once we know how to truly forget ourselves, what's left is an extraordinary peace. That peace is all-pervading,

always present. It is up to us to make ourselves available to that. Just like a gorgeous lover waiting for us, all we need to do is to show up for that sweet rendezvous. Can you believe that forgetting oneself is all that we need to remember? Can you laugh at this paradox? In such laughter we are able to see our clinging to outer and inner reference points. Longchenpa said, "All things in human life are so transient, like the crazy hallucination of a madman, or like being in a dream. Thinking about it makes me laugh." This kind of inner laughter brings about a deep sense of relief.

In the ultimate sense there is nothing to be done except to learn how to enjoy life. That may sound really simple. It's also totally ordinary too, because there is nothing spiritual about it. It's not about lofty spiritual attainments but to enjoy life does not mean becoming decadent either. Enjoying life is accompanied by having a spirit of celebration and joy in all of the myriad manifestations of life. With that attitude our life becomes graceful and the radiance of that inner peace flows freely. That gnawing thought, "It's hard to be human," finally leaves us alone. When we really know how to enjoy our life then all of our searching comes to an end. Until then we search for happiness, enlightenment, the end of suffering. We search for this and that and the list keeps growing. This endless searching is the cause of pain and agony in each of us, but it is very subtle to the extent that we may not even be conscious of it. As long as this search continues in our mind, there is this subtle sense of pain, conceptual pain, and we don't know how to really enjoy life completely in each and every moment.

The act of searching is a form of habit because we usually don't get what we are looking for. Every time we think that we've got it, it turns out to not be the case, and in the end the search still continues. Now we can begin to see that this whole notion of enjoying life, which sounded very simple at the beginning, has turned out to be not so simple. This is not a simple topic. Buddha called the state of consciousness in which all notions of search come to an end "enlightenment." He called it *nirvana* but it has no locality. It is the right now, enlightened state of our mind in which there is no more effort, no more hope, and no more fear. It's freedom from all hope and fear and we can walk into it right now if we are ready. So it's good to ask ourself, "Am I enjoying my life in each and every moment, outside as well as inside?" This precious life is so short. Every blink of our eyes takes us closer to our death. This very present moment will never return. Let's learn to enjoy each and every moment. We don't need anything from the outside to feel happy and free. When we drop all of our painful effort to attain something, then suddenly there is spaciousness in our consciousness, a sense of being unobstructed, and we are able to enjoy life as it comes.

One of the most powerful methods to bring about

the end of searching is deep inquiry. Such inquiry can lead us to a breakthrough. We can drop all forms of searching and see clearly how easy freedom is. One question we can ask ourselves is: "Do I need more suffering? Have I suffered enough?" I'm sure 99% of us will come up with the same answer: Yes, we have suffered enough. We want to end suffering right now if there is a method or technique that is available right now.

Is it easy to bring about the end of suffering? Perhaps it is not easy but it is quite simple. If it were easy then everybody would have been liberated a long time ago. It is so simple that when people asked Buddha to show them the way to liberation, he didn't actually teach anything. His answer was: "The way is the true path, the dharma." The word *dharma* actually means "the way," so what he was saying is the way is the way. It doesn't mean anything. Dharma is not a set of belief systems and methodologies. It is not like some kind of infallible belief system that we can adopt and from that moment on everything is taken care of. Dharma is not some kind of technique that somebody can give us the way a doctor prescribes pills. It is not a magic pill, a wonder drug. We can't just keep mechanically doing the same thing again and again, following some spiritual prescription waiting for the day when everything is going to be just perfect—the day our consciousness is expanded, our heart is open, and everything is finally just hunky dory. Dharma is not tangible. If it were a belief system or a methodology then it would be tangible, but it is not. In the end, the Buddha defined the dharma as the act of laying down the burden, and that, he said, is the way.

The higher spiritual teachings are often more vertical than linear. They invite us to be enlightened right now rather than pointing to a goal in the distant future. The Eastern tradition of sitting meditation goes back thousands of years. The purpose of it is to stop our linear mind, which is constantly going in all directions, and to initiate a vertical ascension, and immediate transcendence. Basically, it signifies enlightenment right there and then, not as a means for an imaginary future attainment. This is a critical point, which can easily be missed. Right there liberation will knock on your door, before you even have a chance to search for it. There is nothing mystical about it, because it is the radical act of laying down the burden, the mental burden. It is the right now, radical act of dropping the mind. Dropping the mind is laying down the mental burden. It is transcending the mind, losing all of our mental concepts.

Sounds like quite a ruthless proposition, doesn't it? It is quite ruthless since everything in life we are trying to secure is very much a concept. Everything our mind clings to is a concept. When we cling to any fixed concept it obscures the reality of life in the same way a veil hides the face of a beautiful woman. We draw conclusions about life, which is nothing more than a collection of memories. Then we don't really live life to its fullest degree since there is no spark of spontaneity. We also miss the miracle of life while being absorbed in projections into the future. The future is a nonexisting world, which accommodates any stretch of the imagination. Unfortunately, life does not take place there. Until we realize that we will again and again be disappointed because our expectations are not met when real life presents itself to us. Life cannot be contained in a dualistic frame by judging it in terms of good and bad. What is the use of trying to have control over it? It will only exhaust us and, in the end, it will be nothing more than a great futile exercise. We create lots of agony every day by attempting the impossible. On the other hand, we can float on the current of the river of life without struggling against it. Then life takes care of itself.

There is a deep-seated fear of life because of the unpredictable and wild nature of it. So we are always trying to control and master it and, doing so, we kill it. That fear has to do with insecurity. We are insecure because we think we will not be able to survive unless we have firm control over life. This approach is truly unrealistic. And as long as we are caught up in this meaningless game, we will never know how to embrace and celebrate life, which is the only thing there is to do. Everything else, everything we believe to be real, is simply a mental construct. Until we have this understanding, we are going to continue living in the dead world of concepts. The consequence of this is that we die without ever having lived.

With that in mind, look around. We can see this played out in the interactions and relationships we observe every day. So far, the whole world revolves in this madness. Such madness is even reinforced by many traditional religious teachings that promise a grand prize in the future or lure us into simply worshipping higher concepts. As a result, the exquisite beauty of life is, at best, left unrecognized and, at worst, trampled and despised. We see this manifested in our history and in our contemporary environment. Once a monk asked Buddha whether there is an eternal self or not. He said that he would not answer such a question since it is irrelevant to spiritual liberation. For Buddha, grasping any concept is a distraction from living in the present.

The burden that Buddha was talking about, the mind's burden, is the burden of all of our concepts. What would happen if we just dropped that burden right now? There would be an amazing, unbelievable level of relief. This is usually called "liberation." It's actually a good proposal. It's what we call a win-win situation because, in the end, we don't lose anything. The only thing we lose is misery, suffering, greed, hate, and delusion. So what is the resistance? What is holding us back? All we need to do is drop the concepts, and we already know how to do that. We are actually very good at dropping things. If we know how to drop our car keys, then we know how to drop our concepts. The logic is pretty much the same. This may sound humorous but it is the truth. Dropping concepts is not any more challenging than dropping our car keys. What our hearts long for is liberation and the way to liberation is quite simple. It is not about adopting another belief system or cultivating another methodology.

Sometimes we begin the spiritual journey with a lot of speculation and analysis and sometimes we die in that same realm without having gotten anywhere. Realizing that life is very short and that time is running out, we have to go to the heart of the matter, vowing that we are not going to waste our time. The heart of the matter is this. Sometimes we have to put aside all analysis, all methodologies, all of our spiritual strategies, and just drop all of our concepts. That's pretty much it. We don't spend too much time analyzing how suffering came into existence. Who cares anyway? What is the use of speculating about all of these spiritual matters? In the ultimate sense, speculation and analysis will not liberate us. So if you are truly longing for liberation right now, then there is only one method, the king of all methods, the methodless method, which is just to drop all of our concepts, not later, not in the next moment, but right now. Just drop all concepts. That is the end of all searching. Then we are free to enjoy life as it is, in each and every moment, so heaven is on earth.

CHAPTER SIX

Unconditional Freedom

As HUMAN BEINGS we sometimes may not realize what we have been missing in our life. This is a great tragedy and therefore it's lucky when we finally realize that something valuable is missing. What is missing has nothing to do with acquiring any material possessions or even accomplishing any attainment or goal. What's missing is not some "thing," like a bright object that we find and then show to others. When we come across what's missing, we find that it is almost impossible to express in words. But, nevertheless, it is the very reason why we are on the spiritual path in the first place, no matter what form we are engaging in.

There is this intense longing that is purely spiritual.  It cannot be easily satisfied by substituting a relationship, material possessions, personal power, or any other worldly accomplishment. Prince Siddhartha was consumed by this longing, so much so that he left all of those things behind and began his quest for what he was missing. There is a long tradition of renunciants who give up everything for the same quest that Siddhartha was on, and many of them succeeded in their quest by finding transcendence. It is the *nirvana* of Buddha, the *moksha* of Hindu sages; it is enlightenment as unconditional freedom.

Some people may feel a vacuum in their life, not knowing how to turn their attention inward to find a true answer. Many religious people are often not lucky enough to get to this point because their religion provides them with ready-made answers. These answers help them to maintain their unconscious state. As the old saying goes, "Ignorance is bliss." Maybe that's why Buddha couldn't find the truth by relying on the existing religious forms. The feeling of meaninglessness can be a devastating existential anguish if one gets stuck with it. That feeling should be used as a prime mover of unflinching spiritual inspiration. It can motivate one to discover true freedom, in which the very root of such anguish is dissolved. There is unconditional freedom that we humans can realize as the highest goal in one's lifetime. Many people never think or hear about it. This sometimes sounds very abstract and mystical, but actually it is not mystical. It is as real as the tea we drank this morning, as real as the rock we can touch when we go outside. Perhaps it is more real than anything else. In the end, this is what is most real. Everything else is illusory. This call, which is beckoning us toward the realization of this transcendental freedom, can sound very far-fetched and very idealistic, not to our heart but to our rational mind, which is addicted to the world of sorrow and concepts. Yet such realization can happen at any time.

When we have achieved some grand illusion we often think that it is the best thing that has ever happened to us. In our ordinary language we often say, “Oh, this is the best thing that has ever happened to me.” It is not. Often what we think are the best things actually turn out to be not so good most of the time. When people achieve some kind of grand fantasy that their ego has been longing for, then they hear from others that it is the best thing that has ever happened to them. But in reality, most things that our mind is seeking or that our mind believes, or that it has acquired, are just grand fantasies. Life is run by a series of fantasies, one after another. But when realization happens, then that is the best thing that can happen to any human being.

So, how can we realize this inexpressibly amazing freedom? This is a difficult question to answer because this truth is not like any other truth. It has no forms, no shapes, no colors, no characteristics, no limitations, and even no belief systems. There is nothing to hold on to, so it is hard to sell. That’s why many people are not buying this truth and are busy buying illusions and belief systems. But only through realizing this nonconceptual truth can we discover the sole purpose of life. It is not enough to have simply an intellectual understanding; rather we must have a direct realization of this amazing thing called "unconditional freedom." It's almost hard to imagine a thing such as unconditional freedom and to believe that it exists in the universe in the first place even though it sounds very good.

Unconditional freedom sounds very good but perhaps our mind is already having second thoughts that such a thing exists. As far as it can tell there isn't any evidence proving that such a thing exists. On the other hand, the mind has a much easier time believing in unconditional suffering. That makes sense. Mind says, "Yes, I believe that. I don't need anyone to convince me that that exists." We have no problem believing in this notion of unconditional suffering when it never existed. There is no such thing as unconditional suffering. Suffering is actually totally conditional. Indeed, it is already falling apart. Can you see how crazy this human mind is? It believes in a reality that doesn't exist and it doesn't believe in a reality that is truly existent. No wonder there is so much messiness in the world.

Let's laugh at ourselves a little bit. What doesn't exist is unconditional suffering, even though this fettered mind somehow wholeheartedly believes that it does. And not only that, it is always working hard to continue and maintain this virtual empire of suffering, which doesn't really exist. There is no eternal ground of suffering; it's already falling apart. Sometimes when we just let go of the very desire and effort to sustain the wheel of delusion, it just falls apart right there.

What truly exists is unconditional freedom, and this is not simply an idea. It is something that everyone can glimpse. This term "unconditional freedom" means that there is no longer a ground of misery in our consciousness. There is this firm, unshakable footing in the enlightened world of joy, bliss, and love no matter what is unfolding in our life because human life is actually almost a play of good circumstances and bad circumstances. It is an unending series of stories: success-loss, meeting-separating, birth-death, being healthy and being sick, having an abundance of glory and not having any. But it doesn't really matter what is unfolding in such an illusory play. Our mind becomes completely rooted in that eternal unchangeable ground of freedom. Each of us has access to that enlightened world at any given moment. But first we have to know how to open our hearts and enter into a strange, as well as in many ways, transcendent state of mind where we desire nothing, where we want nothing except eternal freedom.

If we can't live with that devotion every day, sometimes we can find a moment throughout our day where we can put everything aside. We put aside all of our mind's activities, hatred, pride, as well as the stories that mind is constantly fabricating. We even put aside mind's ordinary activities that seem to be harmless, simply mind's chatter, like a subtle noise. We put them all aside and enter into a state of consciousness where nothing is happening. The only thing that is happening is the desire of only wanting one thing, and that is eternal liberation, unconditional freedom. We literally dive into that desire now and then. It's like the ocean; it has many dimensions. If we are able to dive all the way to the depths, a great miracle happens. We finally realize this thing called absolute, unconditional freedom. Perhaps then we find out that this unconditional freedom turned out to be something we didn't really like.

Ego thinks that it sounds really bad to want nothing. It doesn't like that kind of enlightenment because as far as it remembers all of the pleasure it has experienced has come from getting something that it wanted. That's what ego remembers. For ego, all of the joy and happiness it has tasted this lifetime is a result of wanting something. If wanting comes to an end, ego's mind cannot imagine that there is going to be any happiness, joy, or bliss. The egoic mind cannot comprehend it. But actually, the state of absolute freedom is the absence of all wanting; it is the state of wanting nothing. It sounds a little bit boring doesn't it? It's like receiving an invitation to an exotic place. Then when you ask what's there, they say, "Well, there's no hotel, no spa, no swimming pool, no garden, and the food is pretty bad. Actually there is nothing there. Still, you are more than welcome. More than that, we have been inviting you and trying to get you to visit this exotic place from time immemorial." That sounds quite strange, doesn't it?

The best, the most direct way of describing whatever you might call *nirvana*, enlightenment, is actually a state of consciousness where there is no more wanting. There is a complete cessation of wanting. There are numerous ways of describing that enlightened mind. There are beautiful poems, hymns, and *dohas*, written throughout history, attempting to describe enlightened mind, pure awareness. But perhaps the best way of describing it is to say that it is the state of our mind where all wanting disappears. It is luminous mind, which is already free from all conditioning.

Actually, luminous mind is already residing in all of us. It is sometimes unbelievably easy to access that reality because it is always in all of us, even though most of the time it is not manifested. It's like this analogy. Sometimes in the winter we don't see the river. We see only ice. But if we walk onto the ice and listen closely, then we hear the sound of the river flowing under that thick ice. In the same way, our mind is like that cold ice, chained to concepts, ideas, and misery as well. But if we take a moment to pay attention inside, we actually see many subtle signs, many indications, even though they are not always bright and obvious. I am pointing out such existence in all of us, the luminous mind. Sometimes all we need to do is this simple spiritual sadhana, this simple spiritual practice. We just pause. When we pause completely, we already are in the act of looking deeply inside. In that experience of looking deeply inside, all thoughts, all of mind's activities, and all illusion collapse immediately. In one single moment the world of illusion, the world of self, the world of hope-fear, birth-death, actually collapses, not outside, but inside, in the realm of our consciousness.

When we take a moment to observe, then we see this quite extraordinary, and yet very subtle, groundless ground. It's not actually mind. Obviously it is not form, but it is not mind either. But we should call it something; we should give a name to everything so we can communicate. So beyond form, the only thing that our mind can imagine is mind. So that's why we call it "luminous mind." Luminous mind is so subtle that mind finds it difficult to stop and say, "This is it. This is what I have been searching for through countless eons." What we have been searching for through countless eons is actually nothing more than what we discover in the very humble moment, when mind is not expecting a great manifestation. Since its nature is so nonconceptual, sometimes there is nothing that we can talk about. We just wait and wait. We wait until mind stops looking for it outside and naturally turns its attention inward, finally acknowledging that the truth we have been searching for is already here.

This unbelievably simple awareness, the ground of our consciousness, is always there and it is ready to manifest and shake hands with us in the humblest, subtlest manner at any given moment. So when mind draws intention inward and recognizes it, then the realization that we have is that this is what we have been searching for. And in some traditions they use a method called "skillful means," or *upaya*. This can involve a great deal of hardship and purification in the name of spirituality, in the name of the path to enlightenment. And usually the teachers, the masters, don't give the final pith or pointing out instructions because mind is not ready. It is not ready to just decide and declare to the whole world that what it is seeking, the so-called truth, or God, or Buddha mind is actually that pure awareness. Mind is not ready to make such a declaration because it is too simple. Not only that, mind is a little bit crazy too. As we say, mind is a little bit neurotic and that is one reason, of course. Then there are years of training and being on the path of spirituality, which involves lots of confusion, headaches, joy, reward, success, failure, and lots of setbacks, in particular, one after another.

Then one day there is a moment when the master gives us the highest teaching. They use this very catchy phrase, the highest teaching, and the spiritual ego gets very big eyes. And after they give the highest teaching, one of the things that happens is that we feel this sense of ecstatic disappointment. I call it "ecstatic disappointment" because we have so much joy. We know how simple the truth is, how simple liberation is, if we just make up our mind. But it's a disappointment because all of our grand ideas, speculations, and assumptions about the truth become discredited. So that's why it is ecstatic disappointment.

It requires a sense of this almost out of proportion devotion. And it requires a holy master to convince us that this pure awareness is the very thing that we have been searching for because the mind cannot be easily convinced. If some stranger showed up and said, "Hey, luminous mind is the truth. This is what you are seeking.

When you pause, there is naked awareness, the absence of thoughts, the groundless ground that you feel. This is what you are searching for. This is all you need." Would we be ready to say, Yes and kneel on the ground at the feet of this stranger? Would we say ecstatically, "You're right! This is all I need." Would we be ready to be that flexible, and not so stubborn?

It requires that kind of totally out of proportion devotion, going through all of the hardships and finally meeting with a holy master who has this holy grail and is ready to present the highest teachings to us. It requires such a trick. It is such a beautiful deception to finally convince the mind that unconditional freedom is already here.

CHAPTER SEVEN

Melt into Love

It is said that after Buddha's passing away it didn't take a long time before people forgot his original teachings, and started worshipping him as a semigod. They prayed to him to bestow wealth, health, success, and children. Then there came a line of wise enlightened masters such as Nagarjuna and Tilopa. They taught that the true Buddha does not lie outside of us; true Buddha resides in our consciousness. Buddha is also called *jina,* which means the one who is victorious, the one who can never be defeated. There is Buddha in each of us right now who can never be defeated by the force of inner darkness, the force of greed, hate, attachment, and delusion, and that Buddha has no form, no image. That Buddha, indeed, is residing in all of us as our pure, quintessential being.

We must always turn our attention inward whenever we have the desire to seek divinity, the divine, or Buddha, God, or Brahma. This desire to seek something divine happens quite a lot, especially when we are spiritual. From now on, whenever that desire arises, we might want to remember to immediately turn the attention inward, knowing, even believing, that whatever we are seeking is already inside. This is not an abstract idea. So there is a state of being which is nameless in itself, though we can give it many names. We can call it *dharmakaya*, the body of the absolute truth, or the Buddha mind. Whatever we call it, it is totally enlightened in itself. There is a part of us that is already enlightened and that part of us is actually who we are; it is our true nature. There is also a part of us that is lost, that is a little bit miserable with a lot of aches and pains, headaches and heartaches now and then. That part is also easily entertained by glorious illusions; that part of us is *not* who we really are. That part of us is a shell that is going to break down sooner or later, hopefully in the near future.

Most of the time, what we see of each other is the shell that covers our true being, so we don't see each other very well, and we don't see ourselves very well either. Most of the time what we see as who I am, and as who you are, is merely the shell, the divine incognito. The incognito is separated, lost, and disconnected from the inexpressible source, and it is what we see most of the time in ourselves and in others. It is not who we are. This sense of "I am" is the shell. It is not who we are, and it turns out to be the basis of all of the pain and sorrow that we feel in this lifetime.

If we were asked to be free right now, to jump into

the sea of love in this very moment, we might turn our attention inward and try it, and it may not work. Why? Because of a hindrance, a block. That block is the very sense of "I am" that is the false image of who we are. It is the shell that is veiling, covering our true nature. So the goal of all spiritual endeavors is to actually realize the enlightened part of who we are, not sometime in the future, but right now.

As Kabir said, "What you call salvation doesn't belong to the time after death." Many spiritual seekers, monks, sadhus, and renunciants have been looking for liberation or salvation after death. There is this notion that one is going to have a better incarnation in the future, and be born in a heaven or paradise as a reward for good behavior. The mind is always trying to figure out some strategy, a means to catch this very desirable thing called "liberation," "enlightenment." Salvation, liberation, doesn't belong to the time after death, but it doesn't belong to the time before death either. It only belongs to this moment. Salvation, liberation, *moksha*, or nirvana, whatever people have been looking for throughout history, none of them belong to any time. They do not belong to the past, of course, but they do not belong to some kind of fantastic event in the future either. It belongs to this moment, this moment that is unfolding right now.

When we truly hold this attitude, our spirituality begins to change, and all of our ideas about God, Buddha, and enlightenment begin to change. A shift happens. A paradigm shift takes place in our mind and our life begins to change, not for the worse but for the better, not for the better but for the best, not for the best but for the highest.

So if that is, after all, the true teaching, then we must turn our attention inward wholeheartedly, with the willingness to remove whatever is obscuring that wonder in each of us. We must let ourselves recognize and see it in this very moment, not in the next moment, and not in some fantastic moment that is going to happen sometime in the future.

In my tradition there is a teaching or a method called *ngo drö* (*ngo sprod*), the pointing out instruction. The idea is that if you run into the right person, the right master, she has the skill to cut through all of the trappings of analysis, ideas, and theories, the skill to cut through all of the spiritual recipes and show you your divine nature right there on the spot.

There are many techniques and belief systems for attaining enlightenment, and in the end none of them work. But they don't have to work because we are not actually as desperate as we thought. The path is already paved; the road is already clear. What we are ready to recognize is actually already, always, dancing on the stage of our heart. That nameless, wondrous truth, that presence, that awareness, is actually always knocking on our door. It always wants to be in union with each of us.

When we go inside, shockingly we always discover that the very thing that is preventing us from recognizing the most beautiful truth is not really outside, it is inside. There turns out to be a veil that is very thin and transient. The human mind finds it difficult to just lose everything, to just drop everything, melting all of the contractions and all of the tensions and loving all of the expressions of reality; not caring about death, not caring about birth, not caring about all of the ideas about attaining and not attaining, and with an open heart embracing everyone. This human mind has a very hard time; it has a desire to be rigid, contracted, and always lost in this vicious trap of analysis and ideas, with ambitious and arduous strategies and labor, including this spiritual labor. This is mind's addiction and this is actually the prime reason for all of our suffering.

If we can change our attitude a little bit, by simply turning our attention within, we actually don't have to give up any of our desires and aspirations. We don't have to give up our desire for God, we don't have to give up our aspiration for enlightenment; we don't even have to give up our devotion to the guru, because sometimes that is a very hard thing to give up. So let's not give it up. Do not give up any of this. We can go inside, just turn our attention inward, knowing that the guru is inside, Buddha is inside, Brahma is inside, the divinity is inside. And the moment we change our attention, the moment we change that attitude, then our spirituality changes. Our spirituality is no longer this journey on the conceptual desert where we never find the river that we are seeking, the river of love, the river of truth. Then our journey becomes actually not a journey to somewhere but a journey to liberation that is already unfolding in this very moment.

If you have devotion to the guru, do not give it up but remember that the guru is inside, not outside of yourself. In Tibetan there is a most beautiful phrase, *rang rig don gyi la ma* (*rang rig don gyi bla ma*), which means that the ultimate guru is your pure awareness. When we turn our attention to what is holding us back, we find that nothing is holding us back except this really thin veil, just this thin veil. And if we look into that thin veil, we find out that the basis of it is actually this sense of "I am." But if we look into that "I," it is simply a thought. "I" is a thought that runs deep in our consciousness, but it is just a thought, a mistaken thought. It is a mistaken perception of who we are. That's pretty much it.

I heard that someone is using a word, a verb, *selfing*. This verb, *selfing*, is a very accurate description of how we are creating and maintaining the shell-like falsehood of who we are. Most people are actually *selfing* all day. We are *selfing* all day when we are already ourselves. If we look into a mirror, what do we say? "Oh, I don't like my hair." This is *selfing*. Then we talk to someone: "Oh, I don't like this person." Or, "This person has very good manners and I want to hang out with this person. Maybe I can get something from this person." Can you see that we are always engaging in this mental compulsion, this constant *selfing*? And we go to temples and we pray to some kind of divine entity hoping that we will be successful and that we will be redeemed before anybody else. That's another way of *selfing*. It's a beautiful way of *selfing*. It's called "holy *selfing*," but still it is *selfing*. It's another way of constructing this misperception of who we are. It has nothing to do with the truth. It has nothing to do with pure awareness.

So humanity has been lost in this vicious circle, beautifully and dreadfully through eons and eons, this vicious circle which is the process of *selfing*. And, of course, there are remarkable individuals such as Buddha, Nagarjuna, Padmasambhava, and Machig Labdron who knew how to stop that process and set themselves free from that circle. Of course there are many who have had the courage to break that vicious circle in their very lifetime and those remarkable individuals came from every tradition, not only the Buddhist tradition. And you can be one of those remarkable individuals. Why not?

So the true spiritual practice is actually *unselfing*. Most people don't know what that is all about. They only know the process of *selfing*. So most people's minds are residing in this deluded reality, in the reality of *selfing*. They are always *selfing*. And then finally, when we have that wisdom, when we know how to turn our attention inward, we have the desire to find everything inside, not somewhere else. We want to have salvation that belongs always to this moment, that never belongs to any other moment. When that intention is very strong, then there is also attention. Attention comes with intention. Intention leads to attention. And then something extraordinary happens and then we have the possibility to come close to the mind of Buddha, the awareness, the opening heart, the liberation, the taste of the supreme truth. We begin to actually experience all of them in every moment when we have the taste of liberation, and that is the process of *unselfing.*

So when we have experiential understanding of this notion of *unselfing,* that means that we have recognized the truth. We have glimpsed the truth and have realized our true nature. From that moment on there is a beautiful dance that happens in our consciousness. The dance is the dance between awareness and unawareness. It is the dance between *selfing* and *unselfing.* It is a beautiful dance because in one moment we are in the realm of awareness and we are *unselfing* and in the next moment we might be in the realm of unawareness and we are *selfing.* "Now I'm *selfing,* don't come close to me. I'm not so nice anymore because I'm *selfing.* Oh, now I'm *unselfing.* Come here. Let's have a cup of tea because I'm loving, I'm melting. I'm harmless. I'm at peace." It is an amazing dance, this dance between *selfing* and *unselfing*, and this dance will continue for a long time. Do not try to have any hope beyond this beautiful dance. This dance is what we need. And do not try to long for some kind of great, eternal liberation, which does not happen very often. There is no eternal *unselfing*. Do not expect that you are going to run into eternal liberation. It's the idea that you are always residing permanently, uninterruptedly in the realm of supreme awareness. This may exist as a possibility, but do not expect it, because when you expect it then your attention will be focused on that and you will not know how to enjoy this beautiful dance, the dance between awareness and unawareness.

There is an unconscious tendency, sometimes, to fall back into the habit of unawareness, to construct the sense of self. The sense of self is very painful, inside, even though we can sometimes enjoy comfort, pleasure, and security in the realm of the self. But when we pause and look into it, there is insecurity, there is fear, and there is pain. When we feel a sense of comfort because we have acquired something from the outside, some favorable circumstance like making a lot of money or earning high academic degrees, there is comfort. Maybe we realized that we are very healthy, or maybe somebody told us that we are extraordinary; maybe we realized that we are very smart or very strong or very financially secure. There is comfort and it is very easy to be deceived by the comfort because the comfort is actually happening in the realm of self.

But when we take a moment to look at the underlying reality of that comfort, it is not comfort. There is discomfort. There is yuckiness, because pride is very yucky. Any form of pride is very yucky. It's not very delicious. Pride, security, discomfort are not very pure. It's like eating food from a field that has been poisoned by pesticides. Be organic spiritually and do not eat comfort. Get into the supreme spiritual green movement right now. Do not take refuge in comfort anymore because comfort is filled with discomfort. There is a fear of losing everything that you own. There is also fear regarding this false posture that we construct called "I." *I am; I am secure; I am great.* This is already falling apart. We know that. Deep down we know that. So there is this unspoken, silent discomfort and insecurity.

When we meditate and pray, then *unselfing* happens. *Unselfing* is very beautiful because in that effortlessness of dissolving self then the melting happens. This melting is not traditional spiritual terminology, it's made-up, but it works. We just melt. Our fear melts. Our sorrow, our contraction, our pretension, our passive-aggressiveness, and our hopes all begin to melt. All of our mind's strategies begin to melt; our strategy to be successful, our strategy to get whatever we want from God, or our strategy to make enlightenment happen sometime in the future, as if enlightenment is some kind of a thing, some kind of reward. We lose all of these strategies, not painfully but ecstatically, in that moment of *unselfing*.

Perhaps our heart doesn't want to use any words, any language, any spiritual lingo to say this is what we are witnessing. This is very fearful to the spiritual ego because the spiritual ego always needs precise vocabulary and precise measurement because its melting is very wishy-washy to the spiritual ego. The spiritual ego doesn't like anything that is wishy-washy. It loves boundaries. It loves fences and wants to have very strong fences between the Buddhist neighborhood and the Christian neighborhood. The spiritual ego doesn't have an open heart to language that it is not familiar with. So this melting is very wishy-washy but it is the real deal after all. This melting is enlightenment.

So the essence of spirituality is actually just to melt. We melt all of the ideas of who we are, where we are going, and what we are doing. We just melt everything. When we melt everything, what melts is not our true nature but our painful ego. And where we land is this eternal ground, the sorrowless land within, which is always there.

CHAPTER EIGHT

Transcendent Bliss

BUDDHA SAID that he understood the way to escape from the very source of suffering. That was his essential teaching. He said that if we want to escape, there is a perfect island, which he called *nirvana*. He called nirvana the island within. So there is actually a place where we can all go to escape from the mental world of problems. After all, it doesn't sound bad to be free, to arrive at the nirvana within. Of course, this is very different from practicing escapism. This is the opposite of escapism.

Periodically we have a desire to escape from this world, which is seemingly filled with unending struggle. One of the reasons people go to ashrams and temples to pray and chant is to experience the state of mind in which they can feel that they have escaped these notions of reality. Some people escape, not metaphorically, but literally, and they run away from society. There is a place that we can escape to, but it is not outside. It's in each of us. Buddha taught the most direct, exact path to it. No inner limitations exist in this realm of consciousness and it resides in all of us. It's the land of bliss. It's the best island to go to for a vacation if we are ready.

There is a true escape from the world, not the physical world but false reality, this very painful virtual world that our mind has constructed. We are residing in this false reality most of the time to the extent that we forget to see and admire what is actually happening in each and every moment. We forget to listen to the birds chirping outside of our window because we are lost in this virtual reality, which is the creation of our mind.

It is this deluded, mind-constructed reality we want to escape from, and the perfect escape is this consciousness, which is dormant in all of us. It is truly amazing, and it is a source of love. It is where we can have a feast of true freedom. We can feel this limitless truth and there is no longer a boundary. We can recognize the oneness of all things and embrace every being in our heart.

In Buddhism we call this consciousness "the Buddha mind." Please do not think that there is a huge difference in the philosophical teachings of the Buddha and teachings of other great adepts in various other wisdom traditions. They are the same. The purpose of all of the spiritual endeavors is, in the end, to discover the truth and to be free from this unending cycle of problems. We can be awakened to the Buddha mind in this very moment, but the experience of being awakened to the Buddha mind is completely inexpressible. It is bliss, transcendent bliss.

We keep hearing people talk about happiness and joy in spiritual teachings but sometimes there is no mention of bliss. It is possible that many people don't have much awareness of this transcendent bliss.

It turns out that the very experience of being awakened to the Buddha mind is actually bliss. It is beyond joy and beyond happiness; it is transcendent bliss. In Tantric Buddhism this is called *mahasukkha,* which means "great bliss." The reason that they call it great bliss is because the mind can easily mistake the notion of transcendent bliss with ordinary bliss. Transcendent bliss is a very strange bliss. We can completely abide in it and feel a flow of love, compassion, and joy, and not have any sense of being limited or being fragmented. Being this small "I" is a form of fragmentation. It is not a healthy state of consciousness to associate with a sense of self. It is a state of being fragmented, lost, and separated. Transcending our conceptual clinging to the illusion of this limited self is actually utter bliss.

Transcendent bliss is the experience of being freed from all inner boundaries, all forms of bondage. It is being completely free, free to express boundless love, free to express limitless compassion, free to express the highest level of joy in each and every moment. That is the state of transcendent bliss. Transcendent bliss is supreme happiness. It is the greatest treasure of love, compassion, and joy, an inexhaustible treasure. No matter how much love and compassion we share, we never experience the

The prison of concepts and ideas

exhaustion of this inner wealth. Its bliss is experienced from giving away, from opening that inexhaustible treasure; giving away, radiating, emanating abundance to the extent that there is no longer anything holding our consciousness in the prison of duality.

Usually the reason that we can't experience transcendent bliss is because our consciousness is actually chained by this very illusion called "I." It is chained because this concept literally ties our consciousness to the prison of duality, the prison of concepts and ideas. What most people experience is that their consciousness is chained by that illusion.

But now and then there are people who find the so-called spiritual path. This is another quite strange and sneaky way that ego can actually keep binding our consciousness once again to another form of prison, the prison of duality, the prison of concepts and ideas. Transcendent bliss comes from breaking every chain.

Breaking all chains, losing every concept, every idea, sounds very frightening to the ego's mind. But actually when we let go of every concept, we land on this infinite ground of eternal bliss, and that bliss is not some kind of religious or mystical experience, some altered state of consciousness. That bliss is not the result of doing something to our consciousness, rather it is the pure state of our consciousness.

It is boring when we are lost in concepts. It is much

more lively and much more fun to be free of all limitations and to love the great truth that never can be expressed in any words or concepts. That truth doesn't belong to any group of people, any spiritual seekers. It is the essential truth that thousands of scriptures have been trying to express.

With boundless love toward all beings, we dance each and every moment in the sea of god, in the sea of the truth. And to the extent that we become that bliss, limited consciousness dies. We are no longer bound by our previous, limited notion of "I," the one who is fragmented and has become completely rigid with mind's limitations, hope-fear, right-wrong, good-bad, and so forth. In the end, this is the goal of all spiritual endeavors.

To experience transcendent bliss means to go beyond all limitations. The way is utterly simple as well as ecstatic too. The way to the Buddha mind is the Buddha mind. Of course this is not a very rational answer. The way to the Buddha mind is the Buddha mind itself. There is a very nonconceptual way of entering into the Buddha mind in the very moment we have the aspiration to realize it.

This beautiful quotation from one of the Tibetan masters reveals the perfect way to be in the realm of Buddha mind right away: "This present, unobstructed mind is the ever excellent, eternal Buddha within. Yet its essence is empty and luminous." This verse tells us that the moment that we want to discover Buddha mind, the consciousness of union within, all we need to do is realize that it is already present in our consciousness. So that means we find the way to the Buddha mind in the present mind. We look at the present mind. How simple it is.

When we stop and pause for a moment while looking at the present mind, we feel a shift take place. In that moment we feel an amazing dissolution. Every previous notion of reality just dissolves into nothingness and there is the unobstructed, unhindered Buddha mind. We keep residing in that unobstructed, pure, luminous mind, and realize and discover that this pure awareness, this unobstructed present mind, turns out to be a great source of love, turns out to actually be the inexhaustible treasure of enlightenment. It is utterly simple.

For some people, saying look into your present mind doesn't mean too much. But this instruction is the key. This is the golden key to unlock the great entrance to enlightenment because, beyond this language, the way cannot be taught. This language is the most precise, the most accurate language to describe the perfect way to the final union with Buddha mind. Beyond this language there is no precise language. This language is precise when we are no longer looking for conceptual teachings. It is precise when we open our hearts to nonconceptual teachings, teachings that do not focus on giving more beautiful thoughts and ideas, but rather focus on giving a taste, an experience, a glimpse of nirvana, the island within.

CHAPTER NINE

Relaxing the Mind

YOU ARE CONSCIOUSNESS and so am I. Consciousness is said to be groundless because it has no size, color, shape, or location. Some people think that consciousness is living in us. However, such a view is very limited in scope since this consciousness is all-pervading. We live in it. We are it. It enjoys eternal play. Now and then consciousness forgets that its play is its own manifestation and gets lost in believing that it is separate from itself. That forgetfulness is the fundamental delusion that gives birth to all troubles, problems, and struggles in unending chain reactions. Since consciousness itself is not separate from enlightenment, consciousness being aware of itself can happen suddenly and break the chain created by our forgetfulness.

In the grand play of consciousness both delusion and awareness happen. When awareness takes place, then there is liberation, opening of the heart, and love. But when there is delusion, then the nightmare of sorrow begins. But in the end there is only consciousness, so both enlightenment and imprisonment, happiness and suffering, happen in the realm of consciousness. Such awareness is the only way of liberating oneself from delusion, which is the forgetful, unaware dimension of consciousness. Once consciousness is deluded, it takes the right combination of external and internal conditions for its awakening; for instance, connecting with an authentic guide and spiritual path. For this reason, we see that in all the ancient sacred traditions the relationship between master and student has an essential role.

If we meet a true master who does not want anything except for us to wake up, they will become the clear mirror which reflects our own original face, our pure consciousness within. The true master never gives us anything. They will never tell us that they are our personal savior. They simply create the climate for us to let go of everything we are not, so all that is left is our pure being. Whenever we find such a true master, we can count ourselves very lucky.

If we keep longing for the truth, wholeheartedly, the true master will find us. The master will appear in many forms, including circumstances and challenges, like the story of someone being awakened to the truth by overhearing the recitation of prayers. On the other hand, if we are looking for security, approval, and belief systems, most probably we will run into the wrong kind of master. Then we will be enslaved instead of being set free. When we are doing that, we are not aware of it. Usually we are looking for those things unconsciously. We are like sleep-walkers heading straight for a cliff.

Having a daily spiritual discipline is very important for those who seek enlightenment. There are many sadhanas, or spiritual disciplines. Often they are in the form of a particular meditation methodology, but they can be without form too. They will help us to bring about awareness of our unconscious habits and processes and make them transparent so we can see through them. In the light of such awareness, all the darkness dissipates naturally and our innate enlightened qualities shine without having to improve on them in any way.

Even though we may have a life-changing spiritual epiphany here and there, yet the mind remains pretty much habituated, deluded. Mind has to be purified and sadhana is the method of purifying one's mind. This human mind is shrouded in the layers of unconscious habitual patterns. The moment we recognize what they are, they lose their power because the secret of how they are created is revealed. This is what is meant by the purification that Buddhists talk about. The true sadhana is the practice of resting as the witness instead of being oblivious to the mind games that we play. Many ancient masters stated that without carrying sadhana in one's everyday life, such purification is not really possible, even though one may have those extraordinary glimpses of truth.

Of course ordinary people, those who are not monks

and nuns or yogis, can sometimes have a high spiritual epiphany, which is a very wonderful thing to witness, but it doesn't change our life so much. We can simply tell each other that we have glimpsed the truth. It is the highest form of bragging. If we have nothing to brag about then we can brag about our spiritual awakening. In Mahayana Buddhist circles, people often claim that they have had a genuine spiritual epiphany. Those claims are very authentic. They are not making it up. People have genuinely glimpsed the truth, emptiness, oneness, because truth is not very far from us. But most of the time we realize that we are lost in a world of concepts and ideas. We find ourselves constantly struggling, swimming in the sea of delusion, sorrow, anger, hatred, loneliness, insecurity, comparison, and competitiveness. Some human beings do not find much peace and serenity to enjoy in their lives and yet this whole notion of happiness-suffering, enlightenment-imprisonment is nothing more than simply the grand play of consciousness.

Buddhism teaches that the root of all of our problems is not anything but the state of consciousness called *avidya*, original ignorance. This gives a sense of relief because we don't have to fight an evil empire called "original sin." We simply have to deal with original ignorance, which is a form of forgetfulness. This forgetfulness manifests because consciousness forgets that the myriad of manifestations, this whole notion of reality, is simply its own play. Whenever consciousness falls into this forgetfulness, it keeps getting tighter and tighter and more contracted until all spaciousness is lost, and we find ourselves in hell. This hell has no end until we realize that it is of our own making.

The Tibetan master Tsangpa Gyari said, "The great bliss will follow those who know how to relax their mind." The great bliss that he was talking about is the pure joy, which is life itself, the existence that constantly showers us with its blessings. For this reason the art of attention is considered one of the most powerful sadhanas. It makes us aware of each moment without judging or grasping. In that space, consciousness relaxes and awakes. It is the state of mind that is not lost in thoughts and emotions, where we shift our center from ego identification to pure witness. Sometimes it happens by focusing on a certain object, such as the gap between thoughts. It has the quality of not being hypnotized by the flow of thoughts. Instead, one is immersed in the oneness of being. In the realm of such individual attention, a great metamorphosis takes place. Suddenly, sorrow turns to joy, hatred turns to love, and darkness turns into illumination.

The opposite of attention is the fixation where we indulge in the mental world and confine ourselves to contracted states of consciousness, like pain, sorrow, and the agony of emotional distress. When this mind is contracted, samsara (or the world of suffering and struggle) comes into being out of nothingness. Just imagine that the sky is blue with no clouds. Then, strangely, thunder, hail, and lightning just happen out of the blue sky. That seems strange but that is what happens whenever there is suffering in our consciousness. It simply happens from the fact that our mind becomes very tight, tightened with thoughts, ideas, and emotions.

Buddha himself taught that art of attention as the most timeless and direct spiritual practice. It is beyond all religious affiliation. It transcends all belief systems and belongs to all humanity. Buddha taught that there is right attention and wrong attention. The latter one is merely a form of fixation or, in the worst case, obsession. It will keep us bound to the world of illusion, where we repeat the same mistakes over and over again. If our mind believes that there is something wrong with the way things are, or something is wrong with us, or our clothes, our car, our life, our hair, then the moment we pay attention to that, to what went wrong, suddenly there is sorrow and the world of suffering comes into being. And when we don't pay attention to it, it's all gone. There is no longer a ground of suffering. So there is unenlightened attention. It's the mind's effort to keep constructing the virtual world of suffering and conflict. That unenlightened attention is based on primordial forgetfulness, not recognizing that all notions of reality, as well as all of those myriad experiences that we are witnessing, are simply the mischievous and divine play of the grand consciousness.

Can we simply stop being fixated on our problems or imaginary realities? We can, but on its own mind doesn't know how to stop being fixated on problems. Therefore, sadhana begins with practicing enlightened attention. Sometimes the sadhana is very precise, it has form and structure, like paying attention to our breath, or paying attention to sound. These can be very effective methods to help us to stop engaging with unenlightened attention, the attention that is the force and energy that cause and perpetuate mind's contraction, samsara, based on primordial forgetfulness.

In the ultimate sense, the highest object of attention is actually this inexpressible, nonconceptual truth called "emptiness." It is the ground of all things. So the highest sadhana, the supreme sadhana, is the cultivation of the awareness and attention. Sometimes when we sit in the early morning, we pay attention to our breath and perhaps experience that sudden dissolution of thoughts. We are brought to nonconceptual truth. But in the ultimate sense, the object of attention is not separate from awareness itself, the ground of all things. We are in it, we are part of it, and everything is happening in it—sorrow and joy, samsara and nirvana. Everything that is happening right now—traffic, people going back and forth, rivers flowing, insects crawling, somebody getting married, somebody climbing a mountain—everything is happening in that ground, which is the ground of all things. The absolute truth is beyond the domain of the thinking, conceptual mind. It can't understand it. It can speculate. It can elaborate numerous, beautiful, profound assumptions about it, but it can only really directly experience it.

It's like this. The mind can think about pure nectar and come up with a lot of assumptions about it. But until one tastes the flavor of pure nectar, the mind can't understand it. Just like that, the ground of all things is nonconceptual, beyond words and concepts, and yet it can be realized right now, even in this very moment. But we have to rise above the limitations of the conceptual mind.

The ground of all things is beyond words, but if we use words to describe it, then all we say is that it's perfect. It's beautiful. It's holy. It's paradise. It's the garden of compassion. It's the land of love. It's the river of awareness. It's all perfect. It's all amazing. It's all good. That's all we can say if we try to describe that indescribable majesty of the ground of all things. It is untouched by the primordial forgetfulness, so it is untouched by sorrow and suffering and so it is the land of joy as well. That is the highest object of attention. Can we simply pay attention to that ground of all perfection right now, in this moment?

If we somehow know how to pay attention to that, the ground of all perfection, right now, that means we are experiencing *prajna*, the direct seeing, the direct realization of the truth. That state of our consciousness is the mind of Buddha, the awakened mind, pure awareness. So in that sense, as an idea, the highest sadhana is to constantly pay attention to the ground of all things, which is utterly perfect as it is. And if one doesn't know how to go straight into that ground of all things, then one can begin practicing the sadhana of attention, which means to pay attention to objects or things that take your mind away from inventing and continuing problems.

Therefore, in Buddhist teachings much emphasis is placed on the art of attention, attention to breath, attention to sound, attention to sacred images, or attention to movement—like the river flowing, the leaf on the tree that is dancing and flying in the open air, the birds which are chirping, and the pause between sounds. So this is a practice that requires much diligence. Through unflinching diligence, zeal, and practice, we develop love and passion for this liberating sadhana, the art of attention and awareness. When love and passion arise in our heart, we go through amazing stages of inner evolution. Then, sooner or later, our attention goes through an evolution. It is no longer based on effort. Our attention is no longer based on asserting effort to pay attention. It becomes the natural flow of awareness inside of us. We begin to see what we call the dawn of enlightenment. We may not be there yet, but we see that we are doomed to freedom.

CHAPTER TEN

Glimpsing the Truth

MOST OF THE TIME the very notions of reality that we believe in are actually a fabrication of the mind itself. The mind weaves the fabric of samsara, the world of suffering within, and it takes on its own life and dictates all of our experiences. The thread of this fabric can only be cut by a conscious effort. The continuity of this thread is the psychological force that is manifested in the form of this unceasing craving which keeps the whole process going. It is the energy that spins the wheel of suffering. Buddha taught that this craving is one of the links which chain us to the illusions of egoic existence. But when we look at it closely, we find it to be irrational most of the time, so there is no end to it.

Craving has many forms. It spans the scale from extreme attachment to extreme aversion, with all of its myriad nuances in between. If we take a moment to look honestly into the depth of our mind, we may see that there is a continuous craving—we want this and we don't want that. Of course the object of wanting and not wanting

constantly changes. This craving is the source of much suffering, but the truth is that most of the things that we crave right now don't exist in the way we think they do.

We cannot see the way things are as long as our mind is not awakened from its own delusion. There is a veil preventing us from seeing clearly. It is the basic ignorance that comes along with our existence, and it is perpetuated by the power of craving. When we look into this ceaseless craving, there is a deep sense of being incomplete; because of that there is also gnawing dissatisfaction, which causes us to grasp on to anything that we perceive to have the power to make us happy. We crave sex, entertainment, and food to the extent that we become addicted to them. There is this consistent feeling of an inner vacuum that we try to numb with those things. As a result, we also become obsessed with status and position because they promise easy access to the above. Of course there is a distinction between the natural needs of the body and this craving that we have described. When we are hungry, we eat. When we are tired, we sleep. That is natural. These natural needs can be satisfied, whereas craving generates more of itself. Who is craving? It is the sense of the self that we are completely identifying with. Yet it is the biggest delusion. It serves as the basis of this unawakened life, while it is just a fragment of our imagination.

There is a profound insight that can occur the moment there is a break in the continuation of self-grasping.

This insight is the direct seeing of the truth, the way things are, the great emptiness. We sometimes develop a belief in Buddhist notions like emptiness, transcendent reality, or a belief in the oneness of all things. To believe in the oneness of all things is perhaps the best belief we can have, if we are looking for a belief. But belief itself is still conceptual knowledge, and with that one is still bound to the egoic mind.

Sooner or later we have to go beyond that belief to directly experience the oneness, the ultimate truth, the essence of the timeless teachings of Buddha. Then we experience joy, freedom, and liberation. They are no longer abstract ideas; they become quite real in our personal experience—like tasting honey or listening to pleasant music. In the same way, unconditional happiness, peace, joy, and all of the wonderful words we have been hearing in the spiritual teachings suddenly become quite real.

There is a glimpse of the oneness that can unfold right now. This has to do with the fact that oneness is always here, and freely available. It is the source from which all things arise, and the home into which all things dissolve. It is the ground of everything—life, death, openness, contracting, happiness, sorrow, light, darkness. It's actually here, right now. It's here and it's over there. It's everywhere. It is intrinsically holy in itself, not in a dualistic sense, not holy versus unholy, but holy because it is perfect as it is.

There are two schools of thought. One says that it takes a lot of preparation before we can even glimpse this ground of all things. Another school of thought says that actually we are always ready to glimpse it. Let's take the side of the latter school of thought. When the great Buddhist masters describe the highest level of meditation, they always say, "Do not follow the past. Do not anticipate the future. Relax. Leave your mind alone as it is, and then the supreme liberation arises on its own." What they are saying is that there is an immediate way that we can glimpse this transcendent ground that we are speaking about, the emptiness-oneness. If we simply let go of the memory of the past, and do not anticipate the future, and leave our mind alone as it is, then the oneness reveals itself because we got out of the way.

What the masters are saying is that there is always readiness in each of us to glimpse this transcendent ground, the emptiness-oneness. They are saying that the supreme meditation is the art of resting in the natural state of mind. There is always readiness in each of us to glimpse the truth, because it is not far from us. It is so close to us that we can't even say that it's close because if something is close it means that it is separate. The ground of all things is not separate from us. We are already it and it is also who we are. We are all one. So we don't have to go any place to look for it. When there is total readiness and surrender, we can glimpse it right now, on this very spot.

When we rest in the present moment, a space reveals itself. It is an inner space that is unoccupied by the cloud of thoughts. Without witnessing that space, it is hard for the mind to see beyond its own interpretation of reality. This mind fabricates something and then tries to seek it. Mind creates something and then tries to get rid of it, just like the illusion of self. Mind creates the illusion of self and then mind also tries to either maintain it or get rid of it. Mind creates suffering and then tries to get rid of the suffering. But mind does not know that the suffering is its own creation.

When we leave mind alone, we arrive at a point where mind dissolves and where we know nothing and we are left innocent like a newborn child. Then the ground of all things reveals itself. Emptiness reveals itself, just like when the clouds move away, the majestic mountain reveals itself. Then we glimpse the ground of all things without any veils, barricades, or walls between our consciousness and the truth itself. We glimpse it just as we glimpse everything around us. Then absolute truth is transparent, immediate, and luminous. But glimpsing the truth is just the beginning of our unfolding process of inner awakening. What is required is recognition of the truth, and that recognition is the supreme realization that liberates us.

Imagine that every morning we walk past a garden with many exquisite flowers. We catch a glimpse of them every time we walk by. Then, one day, we stop and start chatting with the gardener who invites us into the garden where we fully enjoy the fragrance and magnificence of it all to the fullest. Just like that, the glimpse of the truth is the invitation to enter into it so we can be fully immersed in it and live in it.

We can be quite shocked at how easily we can catch this glimpse. All we need to know is that this very moment cannot be any better than it is right now. In this understanding, everything drops away right there, our hopes, fears, and projections. That is the glimpse of the truth. That is why the great masters of meditation put so much importance on the gap between thoughts. They taught that the absolute truth, liberation, can be found in the gap between thoughts. They are placing emphasis on the gap between thoughts because in that place we can glimpse the truth. But it doesn't mean anything until there is recognition of the truth. Thousands and thousands of beautiful glimpses of the truth may visit us, yet its recognition can easily elude us. We must have that experiential, nonconceptual recognition of the truth. Conceptual recognition of it is just more intellectual knowledge, which doesn't cure the illness.

Nonconceptual recognition, called *prajna* in Buddhism, means supreme insight, supreme wisdom. It is the direct experience of the truth with unshakable confidence, which has no more doubt about it. Sometimes this nonconceptual insight arises on its own, and sometimes we need a master, someone in whom we have great trust, to keep pointing us again and again to the truth. Otherwise, this journey of looking for truth becomes endless. "I have been looking for the truth last year. I am going to look for the truth next year and I am going to die in my bed while I am looking for the truth." This is not a bad way to die. But many people die while they are still looking for the truth. Their head becomes a spiritual library to a certain extent. They accumulate concepts and knowledge and never really come to this moment of deep knowing. They never say, "Now I know. I know intimately what emptiness, the ground of all that is."

Whenever our mind is no longer conditioned by thoughts, when mind is resting from constantly producing illusions, the world of sorrow, then there is true restfulness, a true inner break. Then we will glimpse the truth. At some point we know the truth without any doubt, and that deep knowing can be extremely liberating. We can say that finally we have achieved everything we were trying to achieve. Finally, we have decoded the great mystery. Finally, we have realized the meaning of life. Finally, we learned from the buddhas the way to acquire unconditional happiness. Then a sudden change happens; unconditional happiness comes to us. Until that moment, happiness is always outside. We have to look for it; we have to produce it. But from that moment on, a divine

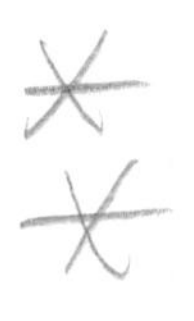

spring of happiness has suddenly erupted and we cannot contain it. We have to share it with the rest of the world.

This is not what most people experience. Most people are going around looking for happiness and trying to produce it. Trying to get something they don't have. But happiness cannot be achieved by finding something outside. Rather, it radiates and unfolds from within, from this inexhaustible source. Once we have that direct recognition of the truth, then we literally feel a divine spring of joy, love, and compassion erupt in our heart. We can't contain it; we must share it.

The most amazing and strange thing about awakening to the truth of oneness is that there is no such thing as oneness as an isolated phenomenon. It is just the absence of an illusory separation between oneself and the rest of the world. When we wake up spiritually, nothing really changes. We are still breathing; trees and mountains are still there. The only thing that changed was the disappearance of all delusions of duality and the suffering generated by them. After that, we are able to find joy in even the smallest things. It seems like we won the whole universe in the lottery.

CHAPTER ELEVEN

Crazy Love, An Ecstatic Way of Transcending Mind

THE HEART OF Buddha's teaching is that everything is sacred. Everything that exists, from the vast sky to the tiniest, most insignificant speck of dust on the ground, is sacred. This is how the world appears to the enlightened mind. It sees the oneness of all in the ground of sacredness. Unenlightened consciousness makes a distinction between what is sacred and what is not sacred, what is divine and what is not divine, what is pure and what is not pure. This is how it relates to the world. Then we are stuck in a mental prison called "dualism."

Many of the existing spiritual traditions make a distinction between the world of the unmanifested and the world of the manifested. The unmanifested world is taken to be this unseen, pure ground from which all things arise. They define this world of the unmanifested as sacred, but they have a little bit of a problem seeing everything in the manifested world as sacred.

Spiritual practitioners often very devotedly worship the world of the unmanifested as either God, or the oneness of all, or the self, or the supreme consciousness. They know how to worship and love the unmanifested world but they don't know how to worship and love the world of the manifested, the world that is around us, everywhere, the world of form and sound. This is the world of everything we can see and touch, the beautiful flower blossoming in the spring garden, the dry leaves brought by the outside wind, and the human body with all of its frailties.

When we can't love both the world of the manifested and the world of the unmanifested, then we are lost in this mental world of dualism and, as a consequence of that, we never see how things really are. This dualism will keep veiling our mind again and again until there is a strong call inside to wake up. When this call happens to us, it is a sign that we are going through the most powerful evolution of consciousness.

The mind that sees the enlightened nature of all things is called in Tibetan Buddhism *dag nang* (*dag snang*). Its literal meaning is "sacred outlook." This is not simply conventional religious thought. This kind of mind is what people call mystical experience. Actually, this is the only true mystical experience that there is. The truth is not another mumbo-jumbo belief, or one of those beautiful hallucinations that people come across when they have a wild ride in the psychic world. When our mind is unveiled, this truth will be as clear as the palm of our hand in front of our eyes. Enlightened mind is beyond duality. Enlightened mind loves and embraces everything, form and formless, manifested and unmanifested, pure and impure. The notion of sacred is not an idea or a theory, it is an experience.

Of course it is easy for our mind to turn the notion of sacred into another theory, another concept, especially when we use the word "sacred" without having a direct experience of it. Sacredness should be experienced rather than just held as part of a belief system. When it is a belief system, then instead of instantly helping us experience the ultimate truth, it actually obstructs our direct entry into the ultimate truth.

One time a woman told me that she has been on the Buddhist path for many years, but she never quite understood the Buddhist concept of the sacredness of all things. She asked me to explain it. This was difficult to answer from the top of my head. No matter where I looked, I couldn't come up with even one word that would logically explain it. Then she told me that one day she watched her son collecting things that had washed up on the seashore. They were precious jewels to him. At that moment she thought that perhaps we could understand the sacredness of all things by seeing through the innocent eyes of a child. All I could say to her was, "Yes, just like that." Remember that this truth is not something that our intellect fully grasps. The only way we can understand it is to drop our mind for a moment and let it reveal itself to us.

We may wonder why there are endless volumes written throughout the ages on this subject when it is beyond words. That's because it is necessary to use concepts and words to point out something that transcends all concepts and words. Otherwise we could not approach this truth in the first place. There are two ways of elucidating the ineffable in spiritual traditions; one is through negation and the other is through affirmation. Buddha used both. He often used the language of negation and his teaching is often found quite challenging. He negated the existence of a creator, the existence of a self, and the existence of duality. He was a master of revealing the falsity of cultural and religious myth. Many people found love in his teachings, the language of affirmation, in his teaching that everything is sacred. The teaching that our true nature is already divine. The two languages seem contradictory, but they both point out the same truth. When we simply drop the illusion of "I," we discover that we are one with everything in the world of all-pervading sacredness.

We are not talking about worshipping something, or treating something as sacred, based on a belief system. We are talking about sacred as a true experience, an egoless experience. This sense of sacredness is simply utter love, love without discrimination, complete egoless love. This utter love goes beyond any form of attachment. We can call it "divine love." It is a very strange love, a love that we cannot compare with ordinary love.

We experience many forms of love in our lifetime and some forms are quite ordinary. We experience emotional love and sometimes that can be rather limited. It comes with mistaken perceptions and attachment because it is based on ego. Divine love is not based on ego. It is crazy love because there is no rationality behind it. It has no reason for loving. It doesn't even have an object of love. It is love taken to the ultimate extreme. When love is taken to that extreme, the ego dies. Ego dissolves in the dimension of crazy love. This crazy love is in each of us. We are made out of crazy love. The very basis of our consciousness is sacred perception, crazy love.

The prime mover of all human suffering, which Buddhists call "original ignorance," begins with one delusion. Our consciousness created illusions, created its own displays and then believed in them as real. It created this magnificent display, a cosmic show—good-bad, bliss-sorrow, self-other—and then bought into those illusions and thought they were real. It's like an author who wrote a fiction, and then forgot that it was a self-created fiction and believed that it was really happening. This whole situation that we are trying to transcend is, in reality, just a story.

Many of us have this feeling that we want to transcend something. We feel that things are not totally OK the way that they currently are. This desire to transcend is common and pervades the hearts of spiritual practitioners across all sacred traditions. We feel that desire and go to a temple, a church, or an ashram to help us transcend. It is of course a beautiful desire. But what do we want to transcend? It turns out to be quite ironic because everything we want to transcend doesn't really exist in the ultimate sense. It only exists as our own mind's display. That is all we have to remember; the very thing that we are trying to transcend is in fact our mind's own creation. We just realize that and get over everything.

When we know how to enter the realm of crazy love, true transcendence is realized right there. Even the "I" who is trying to transcend dissolves. That is the absolute peace that Buddha talked about when he described nirvana. *Nirvana* means enlightenment and its literal definition is "blowing out" or "extinguishing." What is extinguished is the fire of delusion. Crazy love is the holy water that gives rise to a deep sense of relief from that inner burning.

Crazy love is a very ecstatic way of transcending this mind and its ultimate mistake of buying into its own display. We just see everything as sacred and love everything without having any specific object of love. Our ordinary love has boundaries and distinctions. There is what is to be loved and what is not to be loved. This boundary is often quite fortified and many people don't know how to get beyond that fortified boundary. They live within the sense of limited love most of the time. Love without boundaries, crazy love, is sacred perception. It is the only undeluded perception into the nature of all things. Crazy love loves everything. It loves both the manifested and the unmanifested world. It sees everything as sacred. It loves all things that exist, even the most ordinary things, and with a tremendous sense of reverence experiences them as sacred.

Crazy love does not limit our sense of sacred to that which we call religious. It is an attitude that cultivates the experience that everything is sacred. Once we experience that, we can see how extraordinary it would be to live in such a way that we treated every particle, every breath, every being as sacred. When we experience crazy love, we experience love that has no object, no duality.

The question is how do we, in this very ordinary moment, jump into that realm of crazy love? Instead of holding an answer as a kind of recipe, let's keep asking the question. When we keep asking ourselves the question wholeheartedly, we realize that sometimes we need nothing more than a pure aspiration to go beyond this troubled mind. We can go inside and see, once again, that there is no formidable force or opponent. There is just this ego, which is very afraid of opening the heart, afraid of losing all of its protection, its justifications, and its fortifications. Ego likes to hold on to something, it likes to keep

score. It sees letting go of even suffering as challenging sometimes.

When we let go of everything we feel a sense of freedom. We feel this crazy love that is filled with utter joy and fulfillment. Then our step will have dance to it, and our life will have poetry, and the promised land is discovered right under our feet. That land called *Sukavati* is a paradise that millions of Buddhists pray to be reborn in in the future. *Sukavati* means "land of bliss." But that land is not somewhere outside. It only exists in the realm of this crazy love. Do not miss it because you have postponed entering it. When we know how to live there while we are alive, then we have discovered the greatest spiritual secret.

CHAPTER TWELVE

Pure Awareness Is Available in Every Moment

AT THE END of the spiritual road there is nothing left to do. One simply rests in the natural ground of our existence, which can be called "pure consciousness." All spiritual practices are just beautiful distractions if we are not finding this place in ourselves. It is not the subject of the intellectual mind. It is the most enlightened dimension of our being. It is not owned by any religious denomination. If any sect or tradition claims that they have ownership over it, it means that they know nothing about it. The very word "pure consciousness" is only an indicator for this nameless, vast, boundless light within each of us that is who we truly are.

Yet, it is not a thing to be identified with, another better and holier version of self. For this reason, Buddha rejected every notion of self, including *atman* or the higher self. Once every form of self-identity dissolves, we are left with that which is inexpressible, vast, and beyond all limitations. The truth is that we are neither the body nor separated from it. So, what else can we be except pure consciousness? This is the basis of the famous statement made by the Buddhist logician Dharmakirti that everyone can be enlightened since the nature of pure consciousness is luminous.

There is nothing to be discovered as ultimate truth beyond pure consciousness. That's all there is. Every other notion of truth is simply an elaboration of ideas and concepts. Pure consciousness is not the effect of any cause. If it were the effect of a cause, it would simply be another ordinary thing with a beginning and an end. It is present in each of us, and it is not bound by time or space. It is free from everything and it is present in everyone at this very moment. It is the ground of our being, and who we are in the ultimate sense.

The spiritual path is not always straight and smooth, especially if we become deeply immersed in it. We can encounter pitfalls along the way. Many of them can be quite seductive because mind is trying to figure out the highest truth with its old habit of grasping anything that comes before it. We have to be aware of that fact. One of those pitfalls, which ancient masters warned about, is to mistake a pleasant, altered state of mind for pure consciousness. They warned us not to get lost in that trap. We experience beautiful, ecstatic dimensions of our consciousness and yet those experiences can be simply another altered state of mind that has nothing to do with pure consciousness.

We give ourselves permission to enjoy these altered states of consciousness because life already sucks. Life can be very challenging, even meaningless and devoid of pleasure, entertainment, and joy, so why not enjoy indulging in ecstatic states of consciousness? These experiences can become one of the hindrances to the actualization of pure consciousness. We get attached to these beautiful states of mind, and eventually it becomes problematic because we don't know how to easily get back into them. These experiences can be a hindrance because they are impermanent, transient phenomena that have nothing to do with reality and pure consciousness. Spiritual bliss can be a result of the power of one's own mind and outer conditions. Meditation, prayers, techniques, and fervent religious passions can cause false transcendent experiences that can be very addictive to the egoic mind.

Pure consciousness is not a meditative state. If it were a meditative state, it would be something contrived, that is merely the effect of a cause. It goes beyond these experiences. We cannot describe pure consciousness in ordinary language because it is beyond any limiting terminology. It resides in each of us eternally from the moment we are born. That's why it is not the effect of a cause. When we look, we realize that most of the experiences we go through are produced by various causes and conditions, either external or internal. When we see that, we can be certain that we are having a momentary experience, which has nothing to do with pure consciousness. We could be feeling totally fantastic or totally lost, but in either case, there is really nothing there. There is not much underlying solidity in what we are experiencing and our experience keeps changing every moment.

All experience is temporary. It doesn't last forever. Notice that, starting from the moment we woke up this morning, we have gone through a whole range of experiences; some were pleasant and some unpleasant. We have gone through many flavors of experience. We also know that what we are experiencing right now will soon vanish too, either in the next second or within a few seconds. We don't have to do too much to change our experience. Sometimes we simply change our posture or alter the way we are breathing and we feel our experience change into a new dimension. When we meditate and chant inspiring verses, we usually feel quite good, and when we are stuck in traffic our experience is often totally different. Sometimes when we meditate and engage in spiritual practice we feel rather spiritual, but this feeling is not pure consciousness. There is nothing wrong with meditating and doing other practices. After all, feeling good or feeling spiritual is much better than feeling unhappy and depressed or angry. We should remember, however, that these experiences are not the ultimate goal.

In the East, many spiritual seekers have been aiming for inner union with a higher level of consciousness, which is called Buddha mind in the Buddhist tradition. The ancient masters warn us not to mistake pleasant spiritual experiences, no matter how sublime they seem in the moment, for pure consciousness. Even feelings of overwhelming compassion are supposed to be examined. This does not imply that we should stop cultivating the mind of loving-kindness. On the contrary, such spiritual practice indirectly can contribute to our inner awakening, the realization of the supreme truth. Buddha even taught a meditation known as *brahmavihara,* which focuses on loving-kindness and compassion. *Brahmavihara* in its highest form leads to union with Brahma. Such union is nondual awareness, the recognition of Buddha mind. The warning we talked about earlier refers to a beautiful state of mind, which is subject to change at any time.

Pure consciousness is present in each of us right now and we can be aware of it, but we cannot practice it or attain it. We can't attain it because it is already present within us and it's not the effect of a cause. It is not the result of our spiritual practice because it is already present in each of us. Therefore, the only thing we can do is practice being aware of it in the moment. When we say we are practicing meditation, what we are practicing is immediate recognition of Buddha mind. True medita-

tion is direct contact with the enlightened ground of one's consciousness. This level of meditation is what Buddha meant when he said that meditation is the path to enlightenment. For this reason, the profound scriptures of Mahayana Buddhism brilliantly shed light on the subtle demarcation between mundane and supermundane meditation. The latter one is called *sugata's* meditation, in other words, the meditation of those who have gone to unconditional bliss.

We gain tremendous benefit from doing spiritual practices—sitting meditation, sacred movement, dance, yogic and tantric techniques, and so forth. The purpose of doing these disciplines is to clear the mind to arrive at the inner vantage point from which we can see who we truly are. There we will see that we are pure consciousness itself. So they are all very beneficial in preparing us to reach that point if we carry the right intention along with them. But none of these techniques can produce pure consciousness itself since it's already there. It's always eternally there without any cause. There is not even one single moment when pure consciousness is absent. Even in moments when we are totally lost in the world of concepts and ideas, it is completely present inside of us. That's quite ironic, isn't it?

When our mind is grabbed by the force of delusion and ignorance, the lamp of pure consciousness is always burning somewhere inside of us. Whatever helps us become aware of the naturally transcendent state of who we are is the right method, the right technique. If a certain meditation works, then that is the right method. If sacred dance works, then that is the right method. If prayer works, then it is the right method. Whatever works is the right method. The method doesn't have to be Buddhist and it doesn't have to be complicated either. It can be so simple that, perhaps, all we need to do is pause periodically. Perhaps we simply become aware of our breath, or remember some sacred verses now and then. We may not even need to recite those verses. Sometimes all we need to do is simply remember them.

Awareness has no qualities. The paradox of it is very profound, and yet very simple. It can't be described because it has no characteristics, no qualities, no form, and no limitation. It can be pointed out, but it cannot really be talked about. Sometimes it comes naturally to the surface when we are fully in the present moment. When we are in the present moment we are no longer lost in thought or mental projections. Pure consciousness is neither high nor low, neither pleasant nor unpleasant, neither good nor bad. The direct contact with that ground of consciousness is not restricted to mystical ecstasy and such. It can happen in the most ordinary way, while we are just being in the moment, hearing, smelling, tasting, and so forth.

There was a lama in Tibet when I grew up. He was one of those gifted people who never received formal Buddhist training, so he appeared fairly ignorant to the more educated monks. They often made fun of him behind his back, mocking his claim of having glimpsed the Buddha mind. One day they decided to ask him, "What is Buddha mind?" so that they could laugh some more. When they asked the question, there happened to be a drizzle of rain outside, and a bird was chirping. The lama sat down in a meditation posture for a while, and then said, "It is drizzling, a bird is chirping." All of the monks cracked up. They thought he was an idiot. This story shows how you can miss the real thing in favor of lofty ideas. It seems that this lama had a deep insight and genuine spiritual realization. This also demonstrates the immediacy of enlightenment.

Instant enlightenment is quite an old notion in the Buddhist tradition. It is this idea that we can practically stumble across the highest level of liberation in a single moment without any cause, without any process, without any warning. In that instant, we see the true nature of all things clearly, all mental burdens have vanished, all delusions are gone. Sudden liberation, or enlightenment, happens because pure consciousness is already fully developed in each of us.

When we look from an ordinary perspective, every achievement or attainment requires some kind of work. Achievement and attainment are produced as a result of our effort. Therefore, it is easy to think that awakening to that pure consciousness should require a process and that process could take a lifetime, or even longer. But the enlightenment experience happens in a single moment. It happens because it is nothing more than being awakened to what is already here. Once we reside in it, there is nothing else to be done. There is nothing left to attain, not even enlightenment.

Imagine dividing our mind into four portions. The first portion belongs to hatred, the second to obsession or attachment, the third to ignorance, and the final portion is one mind. Most of the time every experience we have is colored either directly or indirectly by hatred, obsession, or ignorance. Buddhists call these the three poisons. When we strip our consciousness of these mental poisons, what remains is a state of consciousness that is not hatred, obsession, ignorance, thought, projection, or habit. What remains as the ground of our mind is Buddha mind. It can be pointed out.

In one of the radical methods of pointing out Buddha mind, the spiritual teacher shocks your mind. The idea is that when our mind is shocked we lose all of our concepts, all of our mental projections, and our pure consciousness, which is already present, is apparent. Once we have this glimpse of sudden liberation then our spiritual practice is directed toward settling again and again in that liberated mind. Eventually it will be an uninterrupted stream of enlightened consciousness. Beyond that there

is nothing else to be done. Whenever there is a moment of being deluded, we can use that moment to practice settling in the very perfect sphere of the Buddha mind without trying to change anything. Enlightenment can happen in the recognition of being deluded.

Spiritual masters used to apply radical methods to shock students into it, right there, on the spot. Those methods can help us have a glimpse of pure consciousness when we are ready. It is already here, when we know how to pay attention to it. It is like the inner stillness, which is always here when we know how to pay attention to it. No matter where we are, no matter what we are doing, we always have an immediate access to that inner stillness. We can find it in the middle of a commotion when we truly pay attention to it.

In the very same way, pure consciousness can be experienced in an instant in all circumstances once we know how to pay attention to it. It is a realm untainted by concepts and belief systems. It doesn't belong to any religious doctrine or school of thought. It is utterly peaceful and it is also insightful, so it sees through all illusions.

Buddha taught a very simple technique using breath and movement to enter into it right away. When we just pause and relax, we find a gap between thoughts. When we reside there, we find the very thing we have been seeking all along. This is the nirvana for those who are longing for spiritual liberation. The sign of authentic spiritual awakening is that we don't want anything else. Then, finally, we figure out that this human life can be ridiculously fun. How could anyone in his or her right mind resist this spiritual awakening? The secret lies not in adherence to any "ism," but in giving in to your natural mystic streak.

CHAPTER THIRTEEN

Ecstatic Compassion

WHAT THIS WORLD NEEDS is a lot of compassion. It is needed in every aspect of our lives. We can see the sad consequences when it is lacking. It is the universal principle that heals when there is injury in the human psyche, and it is the force that unites when there is division. It is the protector of life. It is the warmth of our heart. Ultimately, it is the initial impulse for us to be awakened spiritually. Yet such impulse is not something created by us through effort. Rather it is intrinsic to who we are as human beings. We are born with it. The more awake we become, the more compassion will flow freely. Its quality is like water, gentle and soothing. At the same time, it has awesome power. It is the flowering of our consciousness. It allows us to connect deeply to others, to the point where the concept of separation loses all of its meaning.

There are many metaphors describing the qualities of compassion. One of them is the image of a mother who has so much acceptance and understanding. It allows for all faults and shortcomings, no matter what. In the same way, on the spiritual path we must learn to be compassionate towards ourselves and not be extremely critical and harsh on ourselves. In general, spiritual people can be very harsh on themselves, pushing themselves over the limit and using themselves as spiritual guinea pigs. We try out an endless variety of spiritual techniques and practices to see if they work. Our spiritual ego says, "I have been trying all of these methods and systems of analysis and practice, but they haven't worked completely yet. So now I am going to go around seeking more spiritual information, more techniques, and I'm going to see if they work on 'me,' this 'me.' Hopefully 'me' will be enlightened, 'me' will be holier, 'me' will be more of a saint." This "me" becomes a kind of holy guinea pig.

So spiritual people can sometimes be very harsh on themselves. They sometimes have a lack of compassion and tolerance when it comes down to this endeavor of acquiring enlightenment or personal transformation. They can be very harsh and heartless with themselves because they are constantly using themselves as holy guinea pigs, trying this and that method on themselves to see if they are responding or not.

Have you ever been to a scientific laboratory where they experiment on animals, giving them pills to see how they respond? Spiritual people have the tendency to treat themselves the same way that the scientists treat those guinea pigs. Their heart might be locked, and this is one of the main reasons that people have the problem that they are not getting anywhere after years and years of meditation and serious spiritual practice. Then one day they come to the conclusion that nothing is actually working.

In the process of being so serious and wanting this thing called enlightenment or freedom so much, we literally lose the opportunity to enjoy this extraordinary voyage called our human life. This human life is already quite precious; it is already an extraordinary voyage. It is not something we should miss; it is something we should embrace every moment with love, joy, awareness, and boundless freedom. So the best secret that we can apply on the spiritual journey is *karuna*, compassion, but compassion toward oneself, toward one's own sorrow and one's own delusion.

Sometimes when we look inside we do not find holiness easily in ourselves, other times we do. But there are many moments when we don't find any light, glory, holiness, or Buddha-ness in ourselves. All we find is a bag of neuroses. The main point is not to judge what we find, but compassionately let it be. If it is negative, it will dissolve by itself through awareness. What is positive and good will increase by the same measure.

When we turn our focus inside and see who is there, perhaps the first dimension of mind that we are going to face is not that pure awareness, boundless love, or our true nature but rather this person, the sense of self which is pretty much stuck in itself with hope, fear, sorrow, and an abundance of concepts. It is a very old self. It has been there for as long as we can remember. It has never been dissolved even though everything externally is changing constantly.

Our body is changing and everything around us is changing, but this old self, this sorrowful self has never been completely dissolved and it serves as the ground of all of our old sorrow as well as our new sorrow. That is the "I" that we want to break down, the "I" that we want to transcend. When Buddha was fully enlightened, he said that he had this radical breakthrough, which means that finally this sense of self came to an end and dissolved. Once this sense of small self is dissolved, what we find is not actually a new self, not a new level of consciousness, rather we discover the primordial ground of our true nature, which has been there all along.

When we turn our focus inside, there is this old self that we don't know how to break down. We take it on retreat. We take it to our spiritual workshops. It always accompanies us wherever we go. Sometimes we have a dialog with that old self: "Wasn't that teaching great? Wasn't that meditation awesome? It's working very well on me. This is making me happy. Everything you are learning right now, meditation and the techniques that you are acquiring right now from outside, are making me really happy." That's what the self says to you. And then the old self gets bored with certain techniques and says, "I'm getting bored with these old spiritual techniques. Can you go somewhere else, find a new guru, and learn a new set of techniques?" You see, this old self that has never been broken down is continuing in our consciousness and that has to be completely transcended. But the question is how can we transcend that? What is lacking?

What is lacking is not the intelligence, the diligence, or the zeal. Spiritual people have all of that. What's missing is the genuine compassion that gives room for everything, even the poor little ego that many people are trying so hard to eradicate in the name of enlightenment. Such compassion allows one's sorrow, forgives one's ignorance, and loves all who are not awakened yet. We ourselves can be like the kind father or mother who holds his or her dear child when the child is crying, or has a messy diaper. The kind father or mother has no judgment but instead holds that newborn child with utter love and utter acceptance. Can we hold this confused self in each of us with that level of compassion and kindness, and not hate anything, and try not to create any antagonism?

There is nothing to hate. Even this thing called ignorance is not to be hated, but actually is to be held in that graceful compassion. Sometimes spiritual people have lots of hatred, but it is very subtle. It is very deceptive because it comes from this whole viewpoint of antagonism, that there is something that they are fighting in themselves, something they are trying to get rid of. Have you had the experience that you have an almost antagonistic attitude toward the delusion that you want to transcend, or the sorrow that you want to go beyond, or the suffering that you want to dismantle? There is a sense of harshness that we direct toward ourselves even though we are on the spiritual path, like pushing ourselves to the limit without gentleness. That gentleness is very much needed and then finally we feel this sense of joy in all situations. It doesn't matter whether we are free or not. There is a sense of ease, gentleness, acceptance, and sweet surrender. Either there is a big illumination or there is just a world of sorrow dancing in our consciousness. It doesn't matter. There is this deep ease in oneself because we are no longer harsh on ourselves. We relate just the way parents relate to their newborn child.

When we are sick, we often make sure that we rest and relax. We have a nice soup and cover ourselves with a cozy blanket. We may recite beautiful prayers to ourselves: "May you be healed. May you be loved. May you discover strength." We don't say, "You are an idiot. Get up. Go to work. Clean the kitchen." Like that, when we are deluded we shouldn't criticize; we shouldn't become antagonistic toward ourselves. We must hold this whole world of sorrow and delusion with utter love and compassion since we are utterly perfect, inherently divine, and enlightened from the very beginning.

It doesn't matter whatever the dance of consciousness is in this moment. Consciousness is always dancing. It dances eternally in the movement of joy and sorrow, clarity and confusion, loneliness and fulfillment. It's always dancing. That's what consciousness does. But underneath that illusory dance of consciousness there is an unchangeable, indestructible ground of who we are. And in that nonmaterial realm, in that unmanifested dimension, we are already perfect. Of course "perfect" is still a conceptual word, it is beyond perfect or imperfect but it is utterly perfect. This is the Buddha within each of us. So we must trust, knowing that the ground of who we are is already perfect, is already enlightened, no matter what the dance of consciousness might be in this moment or the next moment. There are many moments when we are fully free and ecstatic and there are many moments when we are lost and confused. But in the times of being confused and lost, we must remember with deep trust and faith that the ground of who we are is already enlightened.

With that deep knowingness and trust, nothing can go really wrong. When we can hold ourselves with both compassion and wisdom, there is nothing that can go wrong. We realize that this lost self, this confused self is actually indeed enlightened, is already the eternal Buddha. We can find a sense of relief, this deep peace, and we don't have to be harsh with ourselves anymore. It's OK not to be free right now. It's OK not to get anywhere. It's

OK that we haven't arrived at the final destination. It's absolutely OK and we can have that big acceptance right now in our heart.

We can also turn our attention to the whole world and say the same thing. It's OK that the world is not free, not enlightened as it should be. And we can have this big acceptance toward the misery, confusion, and sorrow of humanity as a collective society. The spiritual ego sometimes gets very impatient with the world and very angry at the fact that the world is not yet awakened. The spiritual ego sometimes says, "What's wrong with you people of the world? You all should be enlightened. You all should be more compassionate and more wise than you are." And then it turns the intention inside and judges: "I am not enlightened. I'm not this. I'm not that. I'm going to keep pushing myself to become more perfect."

In doing so we end up strengthening and enhancing the sense of "I," the sense of duality that we want to transcend in the first place. The moment we have these ideas about enlightenment, growth, or transformation, which are extraordinary ideas, we have a tendency to use those ideas to judge where we are and our progress on the imaginary scale of spiritual achievement. And the discoveries are always disappointing. The discoveries are so disappointing that we end up challenging ourselves. We become antagonistic, and we constantly criticize ourselves, constantly push ourselves to the limit, experimenting with all kinds of theories and techniques. We lose heart and start applying all of these Buddhist or Hindu techniques on ourselves like we're holy guinea pigs. Then spirituality itself becomes a virtual, vicious circle like a dog chasing after its tail. It doesn't get us anywhere, doesn't lead us anywhere, it just keeps going around and around forever.

When we know how to give rise to this gentle heart, then we are not in a hurry and we no longer have to be antagonistic to ourselves. Rather, we know how to hold this deep trust, we know that the ground of who we are is intrinsically enlightened, already the Buddha, and we have ecstatic compassion. Ecstatic compassion is a very unusual compassion. It doesn't make us feel sorrowful. It is this tremendous joy which knows that things are already perfect. We are already Buddha, yet there is compassion toward this temporary dream of duality. This dream is not going to last eternally. Believe it or not, the universe will provide us with much magic and many miracles to help us wake up. All dreams come to an end. It's just a matter of time.

CHAPTER FOURTEEN

Waking Up to Real Life

ONE OF THE STRONGEST desires in our mind is the desire to put an end to the cycle of suffering. In simple words, we are all seeking the end of suffering; we want to be free from suffering. When we come to the Buddhist teachings we find there is a tremendous emphasis placed on ending this repetitive, vicious cycle of human suffering. This is a really beautiful desire, but sometimes we put too much effort into this striving. Then we are always thinking about ending suffering. We can have that desire for another ten years, or another twenty years, and trying to put an end to suffering is like another suffering. It's like worrying about insomnia: it's worse than insomnia. It's like the fear of fear or anxiety about anxiety.

Still, the desire to be free from suffering is useful now and then. What kind of motivation or aspiration should we hold if not the desire to put an end to the cycle of suffering? The best motivation or aspiration is something called *bodhichitta*. *Bodhi* or *Buddha* means "awakened" and *chitta* means "the mind" or "the heart." It is the desire, the intention, to wake up. This term "waking up" is perhaps the most poetic, the most beautiful word in all of the spiritual literature. Perhaps we can create this enlightened intention when we wake up in the morning.

How beautiful it is to wake up in the early morning and begin to interact with this world of miracles. We hear the sound of the birds chirping and smell the flowers in the garden. The blue sky and the white clouds are dancing; the dark cloud is also dancing. In the morning, in that perfect moment, in that exact instant, our nightmares come to an end. It is such a beautiful moment when we wake up. Perhaps we can compare inner awakening with this early morning awakening. Life begins and it is full of sights and smells.

So the question is: What do we have to do to wake up? This is a very important question. Of course there are many people who do not want to wake up. Many spiritual people, even Buddhist people, do not want to wake up. That's not their main motivation; not why they are on the path. Many people are on the spiritual path with a desire to find a sense of security, psychological comfort, or a sanctuary, not with a genuine desire to wake up. It is amazing that this mind invents fear and misery out of nothingness, and then also invents false sanctuaries, invents comfort, eternal comfort. Our mind is like a computer playing a computer game. In these games we can have enemies and an army and we can have battles with very powerful weapons. But none of these are real;

it is only a virtual creation. This is how our mind works. Mind creates struggle, with all of this fear, loneliness, hatred, and divisions between subject and object. And then mind also creates some kind of sanctuary or comfort. So the point is: not everybody is trying to wake up. If that were true, we would live in a different kind of worldly society.

What should we wake up to? This is a very important question. Of course we can use words like "infinite emptiness." It sounds very beautiful but what does it mean? Sometimes these words become nothing more than beautiful concepts and ideas. Where is infinite located? Maybe it lies somewhere behind a heavenly cloud. Infinite becomes a very beautiful idea, perhaps related to some notion of eternal self. Buddha realized that this was another misleading illusion, and when he started teaching the first thing he did was deconstruct all illusions. Buddha's main message was about transcending and deconstructing all illusions, personal as well as collective. He deconstructed the notion of *atman*, the eternal self, which was a dangling carrot for many people and still is even today. The idea of something infinite can sometimes be tricky. If we mystify and somehow project it outside, then it becomes just another conceptual phenomenon.

So the question is: What does one have to wake up to? And the answer is life. We wake up to life itself. Life is infinite. It is oneness. It is emptiness. It is the wonder of wonders. When I say "life," I am not speaking about the life in our heads. That life is simply an accumulation of story lines, so we are not referring to that life. Whenever we say that we have a great life, we are speaking about the life in our head. And whenever we say that my life sucks, we definitely are speaking about the life in our head. There is life that exists in our head. It is nothing more than reading a story about the life of a character in a novel. It's fiction, made-up stories. None of it is real. That life in our head, the one we grasp and believe to be true, is actually only happening like a movie, like a novel in our head, in our deluded mind. It's not really happening.

The life that we are talking about waking up to is not this usual life that has all of these remembered stories. It is life that is in some sense actually quite mysterious. It is not your life or my life; it is the totality of life. It does not exclude anything; it encompasses everything—the clouds in the sky as well as the bird flying above us. It includes the breath we are taking in as well as the insect crawling on the ground. It includes the dew on the grass in the morning as well as the traffic on the highway. It includes the bliss in our hearts and the pain in our joints, everything we are witnessing, everything we are glimpsing when we are no longer lost in the troubled mind. That is life. Life is actually big. It is infinite. It is boundless.

When we say, "My life is very painful," there is no infinite, no boundlessness in that life. My life is like the stories of characters in a fiction. It becomes very small and very limited. It is filled with ongoing struggle because there is a very small space for love and joy in that mind-manufactured life. "My life" is fictitious. Meditation is all about waking up to life, real life, not artificial, conceptual life, but life that is mysterious and magical at the same time too. It is hard to describe the wonders of life. All we can say is that it is mysterious and beautiful. It is intrinsically wondrous. It is transcendent reality because the rational mind cannot comprehend the inherent wonder, the miracle, and the sacredness of life as it is. And life is already happening, now.

Where are we going? This is a very good question. Where are we going with all of our exhausting effort of trying to achieve something, earn something, accumulate something, conquer something, destroy something, and defend something? The question is where are we going with all of this exhausting effort? We even do this with spiritual matters, accumulating this, acquiring that—this system of thought, that system of knowledge. Where are we actually going? Can we see some amazing destiny, some destination lying in front of us that is much better than the real life that is already unfolding?

Buddha taught a simple meditation which he called "wholesome attention." As far as Buddhist meditation is concerned, all meditation is a form of attention, an act of attention. Attention is a natural ability of our

consciousness. Our consciousness has amazing gifts and one of its best gifts is its ability to pay attention, because the art of attention is the most direct way to enlightenment. This is taught by all of the ancient masters.

Buddha talked about focusing on an object like counting our breaths as the art of attention. Tilopa said, "Use your mind to look into mind and then samsara will diminish right there." Using mind to look into mind is a form of attention. When we pay attention to an object, even a very finite object, it can become infinite because something grabs our attention. It's like looking at a beautiful photograph of a drop of water or dew on the leaves of trees. When we see enlarged pictures of such insignificant phenomena, they are quite often extremely enchanting. Like that, when we pay attention to something that we don't usually pay attention to, our mind stops, and we're pretty much blissed out. So when we pay attention to anything with the desire to wake up, then what happens is that our mind stops for a while.

Our mind, samsara, the ever-spinning wheel of delusion, is not out there. It is in each of us. This is one of the main messages of the Mahayana Buddhist teachings. Samsara is actually a state of mind. This mind is always spinning, lost in its own stories, lost in its own imagination. 99% of our notions of reality are simply inventions and projections of our own mind. But mind is lost and thinks they are real. It thinks that there is a problem that it has to fight against and fix, then there is unnecessary pain in our hearts.

So when we pay attention to something, not in the ordinary sense but with the desire to wake up, then that mind, the samsaric mind, stops. It stops because nobody is spinning that wheel; so when the mind stops, everything stops. All of our struggles and problems stop. Even the sense of "I" stops. All of the veils are suddenly lifted from the face of our consciousness and nothing obscures our mind from seeing the wonder that real life is. Real life doesn't sound as spiritual or as fancy as terminology such as Buddha nature or Godhead. But we will not find Buddhism in our ideas or in our concepts. We will find Buddhism in our real life. We will find Buddhism in the wonders of life, in the trees, in the stones and rocks, in the breath, in the heart, in joy, and in pain. We will not find it in the texts. What we find in the texts are ideas about Buddhism. To be totally lost in these conceptual systems and books is like going to a restaurant and being in love with the menu but never ordering or tasting the food. This is what we do sometimes. And then when we finish reading this menu, we get another menu. It can be a beautiful menu framed in gold, turquoise, and coral. Sometimes we like it because it is very thick and very detailed. But we can get lost in a holy menu in a spiritual restaurant and never order the real food, the real meal, and never taste the *amrita*, the pure nectar. The *dharma*, the true way, is called *amrita*, which means the nectar that quenches our thirst and heals the eternal illness in our heart.

It is sometimes very easy to miss the point but we don't have to. We don't have to miss the point. Finally, we can have this moment of revelation. We can see that when we are going somewhere, we are always going in the wrong direction. No matter how much we keep looking for liberation, for enlightenment, we will never find it as long as we are going somewhere to find it, because actually it is here. Life is enlightenment. Life is the sacredness. Life is emptiness and emptiness is life. Infinite is the finite and the finite is the infinite. Manifested is in the unmanifested and unmanifested is in the manifested. This is the great unity.

So when we pay attention with that desire to wake up, we see that mind stops. There is no magic, no joy higher than this natural stopping of the mind. When mind stops, pain, struggle, everything just stops on its own. There is a sudden relief. In Buddhism enlightenment is called "inner relief," a form of laying down the burden. Mind is actually a burden, and when there is no veil then suddenly we can be awakened to real life and then all of our desires, all of our obsessions of going somewhere and looking for something beyond the realm of this moment, come to end and then there is utter joy, utter love. Not only that, but then something actually opens up inside of each of us.

In the same way that volcanoes sometimes erupt, or a spring suddenly gushes from the ground, something actually overflows in each of us. And what overflows is this inexhaustible, spiritual treasure. Inexhaustible treasure here means that no matter how much you use the treasure, it is never exhausted. It is an inexhaustible treasure of joy, boundless love, and compassion. It is compassion toward all beings for their sorrow, for their confusion, and it becomes genuine and effortless. This natural blossoming of love and compassion becomes effortless. Finally the Buddha within is no longer a notion, but a lived reality that is the core of our being, which is not separate from life itself.

So when we are completely awakened to life, then the Buddha that is dormant, that is hiding in us, is revealed. It is revealed not as another form of self or a higher self, but as this spontaneous, natural overflow of love and joy. Then we begin to see that all of this talk is not just mystical rumor. It is not some kind of abstract concept or some kind of outdated Buddhist idea. It becomes real in our experience and we begin to see that it is actually a timeless truth. And then in that nonconceptual understanding we begin to realize a very important timeless wisdom, and that is this notion that everything is sacred. Life becomes sacred. Not my life, not your life, but life as the totality that we are witnessing right now. Can we witness the totality of everything in this very moment without going through things one by one? Can we recognize that there is a totality happening right now, everything from the blue sky all the way down to the dust on the floor? Can we see that totality as the real mandala, the true mandala, the sacred dimension?

There is a tremendous sense of fulfillment and joy when we are finally awakened to this. We don't say, "I like this sacred dimension, I like this totality, but I want something else." We don't think that this sacred dimension is very beautiful but there are some problems and it has to be remodeled. Our sacred dimension, the intrinsic totality of all things, is inherently perfect and infinite as it is. Can we come up with this lie, this separation between self and other in the sacred dimension of that mandala? Is there someone that we should not love? Is there somebody that we should hate? Is there somebody that we should exclude? So then we begin to see that life, real life, is everything and then we become a true devotee.

A true devotee is somebody who worships life, real life. The mind of the true devotee has devotion to the sacredness of all things. If you are in this state that I am speaking about, then I don't have to explain anything. But if you feel that you are not in that state, can you at least imagine or even pretend that you're in such a pure state of mind? Can you see how wonderful that would be because all struggles, all effort of going somewhere and looking for this and that come to an end? All of our strategies of trying to defend something, the illusion of self, come to an end and we see the infinite everywhere. When we see the absolute truth, the all-pervading sacredness, we see it everywhere. We see it in everything, in the dust on the ground, in stones, in sand, in the breath, in our body and in the body of others, in animals, in the grass, in the clouds, and in space. We see this sacredness in everything. In that moment suffering cannot continue, misery cannot continue, and this exhausting effort of going somewhere and trying to dismantle the disorder cannot continue anymore. This effort finally comes to an end.

In this very moment can we be awakened to real life? Can we love it? Can we see it as infinite, or God, or whatever we have been looking for? And then can we live in that unconditional joy of being in union with God or Brahma, or emptiness, which is the real life? Conceptual life, mind-made life, dissolves in the moment of awakening to the real life; and when mind-made life dissolves, then all of our problems dissolve. Can you believe it? All of our pain and complaints, and whining, come to an end. It is the end of whining.

CHAPTER FIFTEEN

Devotion, Surrendering to the Present Moment

THE ESSENCE OF BUDDHISM is acquiring an enlightened understanding of life. Therefore, Buddhism and life are inseparable. There are many theories about the meaning of life. Some people believe that life is futile and meaningless. They end up being quite unhappy and are always struggling with something, if not with a particular situation, then at least with themselves. Life is this mysterious flow or force that unfolds on its own. We have very limited control. Things that we want to happen, don't happen, and things that we don't want to happen, happen. Sometimes we can make desirable things happen and this causes temporary happiness. But we have very little control over life. Life is not like a car where we are the drivers. Life is not like clay where we are the sculptors.

Sometimes we see people white-water rafting in the mountains. They are having so much fun, but we also see that they have very little control over the raft. Perhaps one of the reasons that they are having so much fun is that they are allowing themselves to ride along with the natural flow of the river. Imagine if they were fighting the flow and trying to go against the stream. That would be very tiring and they wouldn't be having so much fun. They would be frustrated and they would be plunged into the depths of despair every moment. So true Buddhism is a form of white-water rafting in the river of life. It is devotional surrender to life.

What is the most enlightened attitude we can hold in relation to life? A spirituality that teaches us to reject life and look for a better existence in the hereafter is misleading. Many spiritual traditions, including Buddhism, teach that life is sacred. It is not to be rejected. It is to be embraced and loved because we will never discover a truth, a reality, or a oneness that is separate from life itself. We can come up with notions of truth or divinity that are supposed to be more sacred, more holy, and more transcendent than life itself. Then we end up worshipping those notions, but we are simply worshipping ideas and concepts. Concepts have no reality. One day we will wake up and realize that what we have been worshipping is a fiction, an illusion, a myth. We will realize that we have been wasting our time, misleading ourselves. We may come to this very shocking as well as radical conclusion that life is actually everything. There is no grand truth that is beyond life itself. Life is the divine. Life is emptiness. Life is oneness.

Of course, we can love the scriptures. If we are Buddhist we can read about notions of emptiness. We can worship the sacred ideas in the scriptures and think that *this* life is trivial and unenlightened. We can think that the beautiful ideas in the scriptures are sacred. We can think that they are pointing out a reality that is hidden from our consciousness, one that is completely separate from life itself. But sooner or later everything we are aspiring for, everything we have been worshipping, will be realized as an illusion.

An eleventh-century Tibetan master, Dromtonpa, once met with a monk who was doing many forms of spiritual practice, reciting sutras, circumambulating temples, and so forth. The master said, "Everything you are doing is not true spiritual practice." The monk was very perplexed and asked, "Well then tell me, what is true spiritual practice?" The master answered, "Let go of this life." It sounds like he was encouraging the monk to reject life. But what he meant was, do not reject life. Simply let go of all of your ideas about life. Our ideas about life veil life. They are the hindrances to fully experiencing life. They cover life so that we can never have this immediate, sacred contact with life itself. It's like this. When we meet people we usually have preconceived notions about who they are, so we never really meet them. We simply meet with the person that we have constructed. We meet with our own concepts. Most of the time we don't really meet anyone because of our own concepts. We rarely meet anybody and therefore we are very lonely and sometimes confused. In the same way, we have to go beyond all of our ideas and concepts about life to meet it. Otherwise we never experience life. Many people never know what life is because they live through ideas, fantasies, and projections.

Life is totally precious. It is divine. It is the truth. It is oneness. But sometimes we are not ready to recognize that and therefore we have to be a little bit lost, intentionally lost. The realm in which we should be intentionally lost is called spirituality. We have to tell ourselves that we are embarking on a divine journey to some fantastic destination, a journey that has nothing to do with life, a journey into nirvana, or a journey into the great truth. We can stay on that journey for months and months, or even years and years. Then one day, if we are lucky enough, we realize that whatever we are looking for is not out there. There is no "out there." Life is nirvana. This is nirvana. Coming to this conclusion is the great U-turn. Sooner or later we have to make that great U-turn and wake up, realizing that this journey of searching outside is not leading us anywhere. At the same time we must express gratitude for the journey because if we hadn't been lost on that journey, we might never have realized that everything is already here.

The Buddhist master Asanga said, "A master discovers truth through the act of devotion." Devotion plays a very important role in spirituality. Hindus call it bhakti yoga. Many of the ancient sages in India and Tibet taught that path of devotion. It is one of the most powerful, most effective paths to enlightenment. Devotion is a shortcut to liberation because it is nonconceptual. It is experience, direct experience. It has nothing to do with ideas or conceptual analysis. It is the raw experience of being one with the divine, one with our true nature. It is the experience of dissolving the illusion of self rather than acquiring the idea, or concept, of no self. Most of the time when we read scriptures, or think, or have discussions about no self, we are indulging in ideas. They are wonderful ideas, but they are simply ideas. Ideas are very limited. They are lacking in love, humility, goodness, and true surrender. Ideas are simply mental positions, merely mental constructs. They don't take us anywhere. There is a point where we have to go beyond all of our ideas. When we don't know how to go beyond our ideas, we can actually turn those ideas into a way of obscuring the truth.

Devotion is an experience that has nothing to do with belief systems. It is the right now experience of melting the illusion of self and dissolving into the holiness which is life itself. Devotion is actually the act of surrendering. True devotion has no object. Is it possible to have devotion without an object? Devotion without an object is devotion that has no object separate from us. True devotion has no truth, no sacredness that is separate from us or separate from life. It is not out there like some kind of celestial entity residing in a mystical dimension behind a cloud.

So devotion without an object means that there is nothing that you can worship, nothing that you can surrender to that is separate from life itself. There is nothing that is separate from us. This understanding is considered the highest spiritual realization. This is called sacred perception. Sacred perception is the transcendence of all perceptions. It is actually the destruction of all perceptions because all perceptions are colored and conditioned by our own ego, our own dualism and ignorance. Sacred perception is the only perception that sees the true nature of everything, the true nature of reality and life itself.

How do we practice devotion to life? This has to do with completely surrendering to life, being at the mercy of life, having no more hopes and fears, no more wanting this and not wanting that. Not being in control of life, but letting life be our master. Letting life be our guide and surrendering to it completely without having even the slightest desire to control it or to modify it. When we do that, there is no more my life and no more your life. There is only life. There is a big difference between these two points of view: life and my life. The moment we have the thought "my life," there is an immediate urge to control it.

"Oh, my life. This has happened. This has not happened. This should happen. This should not happen." There is no more surrendering; there is only ego's fight. There is a constant battle inside of us. We are always trying to conquer and control life. Then we become completely lost in the prison of hope, fear, and expectation.

So much unnecessary suffering results from simply believing in this notion called "my life." We become very greedy, stingy, overprotective, and overdefensive the moment we fall into this delusion called "my life." We want to defend and secure the thing called "my life" and we see sometimes that a huge percentage of reality is a direct threat to "my life." We become completely paranoid and fearful of reality, of the people and situations we encounter. We also become afraid of death because death symbolizes the end of the so-called "my life." The practice of true devotion is devotion to life. It is not devotion to some grand idea of divine, but devotion to life itself. In that process the notion of "your life" and "my life" dissolves. There is only life.

It's like sitting in the ocean. Have you ever had the thought "my ocean"? There is no my ocean or your ocean. There is only ocean. If there was my ocean, then we might not enjoy that ocean. We might want to kick everybody off of the beach. We might say, "You have to pay, otherwise you are not supposed to enjoy it here with your kids, with your dog." Can you see that this "my" is such a destructive thought? An immediate contraction happens in our consciousness. Maybe that's why we feel so much joy and so much spaciousness when we walk into the ocean. Walking on the beach and dipping our feet into the ocean is a very religious experience, where we are transcendent. It sometimes helps us take our attention away from this egoic mind because there is no more "my." There is no my ocean. There is no my sky, my universe, or my cosmos. There is only ocean. There is only sky. There is only cosmos. In the same way, there is only life, and life is already unfolding.

How can we discover life? The path is very simple, utterly simple. Buddha gave a sermon that he said summarized all of his other sermons. He said, "Do not live in the past because the past is already gone. Do not live in the future because that is filled with expectations and it hasn't arrived. Be fully aware of whatever is arising in this very moment with total awareness and insight. Be in the present moment. This is the pure way to discover life that is none other than emptiness, divine truth, and oneness." Can we be in the present moment? Can we be in the present moment by simply diving into the river of breath or by simply listening to the sound of birds chirping outside? Can we be in the present moment by feeling the dance happening inside our chest, the pulse, the divine dance? Can we bring all of our attention, all of our focus, all of our heart into that pulse and discover reality and life itself?

Life that is free from all of the tenets of our projections and ideas and preconceived notions, life without any barriers. That, perhaps, is like meeting the eternal Buddha. Then when we try to describe life, all we can say is that it is happening in this moment–inbreath, outbreath, space between thoughts, and sensations in our body.

Can we surrender to this present moment? Can we surrender to life that is already unfolding right now? Can we open our heart and instead of waiting and postponing, immediately, in this very moment, surrender all of our ideas of what life should be? Can we surrender the concept "my life" with total trust that life, this mysterious and uncontrollable flow, this force, this existence, is indeed divine? In that moment my life and your life dissolve. There is no separation between us and the rest of the world. There are no more boundaries and limitations.

Then there is only love. There is only joy. This is the true sacred outlook.

A Christian pastor recently told me that he often goes into the woods to hear the voice of God. Maybe the voice of God is actually the voice of life. Life is always speaking to us but we don't hear it. Life is always inviting us to an eternal feast of freedom and unconditional love. Life is always asking us to let go of all of our fear, all of our hatred, asking us to dissolve into life itself. Then life is sacred. Life is actually everything. This is very simple, but very hard to understand. That's why we may have to keep getting lost in spirituality for a while. So please, let's continue getting lost for a while or we can quit being lost and be free, once and for all. It's our choice.

Dharmata Foundation carries the current inventory of Anam Thubten's books and recorded teachings on CD and DVD. For more information visit:

www.dharmatafoundation.org

Anam Thubten travels nationally and internationally to teach and conduct meditation retreats. To obtain a schedule of Dharmata events please visit the website or email: info@dharmata.org

Other inquiries may be directed to:

Dharmata Foundation
235 Washington Avenue
Point Richmond, CA 94801
510-233-7071